'We spend our life in conversations, but so often come away thinking that we could have achieved more from them. Whatever your role or gender, *Workstorming* offers a practical toolkit to increase the odds of getting your conversations right.'
Sharon Doherty, Global Organization and People Development Director, Vodafone

'*Workstorming* is packed with practical insights gleaned from Rob's extensive personal experience, many of which resonated with my own challenges of leading large teams during my career. Rob reminds us that if we listen, pause and focus on meaningful conversations we can be at our most impactful, not only in our workplace but also in our personal lives.'
Ian Buchanan, Group Chief Information Officer, Barclays Bank Plc, and Global Chief Operating Officer, Barclaycard

'Rob understands the dynamics of conversation inside out. He has vast experience and mastery in this field. The world will be better for him sharing it.'
Hugh Brasher, Race Director, London Marathon

'With the pressures of the "always-on" digital age, Rob's simple techniques based on real-life stories helped me become more effective at work. It's easy to feel overwhelmed, but Rob helps you to step back, develop your business relationships and working style successfully, and still enjoy your life with family and friends.'
Bryn Jones, Chief Technology Officer, Three UK

'Rob knows how to have meaningful conversations that allow people to be honest with themselves and authentic with others. I can't think of a better person to write a book like this!'
Paula Vennells, Chief Executive, Post Office Ltd

'Full of wonderful anecdotes, anchored in practical experience, and backed up by hard science, *Workstorming* is an essential guide to being a more effective worker, manager or leade'
James Alexander, co-fo ··········· **·on-to-person lend** ing exchang

D1460882

4 1 0273154 6

'As someone who spends his own professional life advising leaders on how to improve their conversations, I hugely admire the clear and practical insights which Rob brings to the subject. I highly recommend this book to anyone who wants to improve the way they talk to others at work.'
Dik Veenman, Founder, The Right Conversation

'Have you ever come away from a work conversation or meeting wondering how it had gone so wrong? Rob Kendall has an extraordinary ability to see beyond the event itself, provide hidden insights into why it may have happened, and propose easy-to-apply avoidance strategies and techniques. His insight has helped me to deal with challenging work situations that all of us can face in everyday conversations – from large team meetings through to one-to-one discussions. This book is a must-read for those seeking more valuable and rewarding interactions.
Dr Claire Ruggiero, Vice President Technology and Innovation, Lloyd's Register

'*Workstorming* is engaging and thought provoking, tackling the simplest but most profoundly important human behaviour – talking to each other. You'll recognize the life pressures and examples of conversations going wrong, and Rob offers clear, practical ideas and techniques to improve our conversations.'
Bryan Diggins, Group Head of Quality, Laing O'Rourke

'Rob uses his experience to great effect and encourages a focus on how we can get more from our interactions. *Workstorming* captures the numerous challenges of work communications and provides practical ways to help anyone seeking to have better conversations.'
Kay Eldergill, Human Resource Director, Met Office

'As a great believer in the power of small talk, and being a "skimmer" in remission, *Workstorming* offers thought-provoking advice on ways to improve my interactions at work and at home. Taking the time to reflect on the anchors we set is a crucial skill for all business leaders.'
Gerry Mulholland, Head of Health, Safety and Environment, British Gas

'Rob's new book helps us understand why everyday workplace conversations can go so wrong and provides simple strategies for making them more effective. In today's globally connected world, he teaches us that paying attention to the context of a conversation helps us work effectively across cultures and build enduring, trust-based relationships with bosses, key suppliers or team members around the world.'

Sue Jackson, HR Director Asia, Freshfields Bruckhaus Deringer

'In *Workstorming* Rob has managed to achieve that balance between insightful content and an engaging narrative. The use of character scenarios adds context and richness to the content. The book is great timing by Rob, with the quality of conversations and workplace communications coming under increased scrutiny and interest.'

Gary Browning, Chief Executive, Penna Consulting Plc

'As we're bombarded with information and face relentless demands on our attention, our fulfilment and success at work depend on our ability to find our own voice, make it heard above the crowd, and make space to listen. In *Workstorming*, Rob throws light on one of the great challenges of our time.'

Clare Geldart, Marketing and Communications Leader, Global Risk Assurance, PricewaterhouseCoopers

'We have been lucky to have Rob help us grow our company into a leading and award-winning player in a highly competitive market by putting into practice the advice he outlines so well in this wonderful book. By reading *Workstorming*, you too can benefit from that wisdom.'

Philip Dobree, Founder and Chief Executive, BAFTA- and EMMY-winning Jellyfish Pictures

'I first met Rob over 15 years ago when working in banking. He inspired me then and continues to be an inspiration to me now in my very different world, where I am a director of a children's hospice. The simplicity of his approach, which centres on having brilliant conversations, has transformed the way I work for ever.'

Liz Gratton, Head of Fundraising, Donna Louise Hospice Trust

'We engaged Rob to guide us and our joint-venture partner to better align ourselves, listen and monitor whether we were addressing challenges and seizing opportunities. It worked! Rob helps us all get the importance of listening, conversation, saying what we mean and accepting differences and diversity. We look forward to this book helping many other joint ventures overcome the natural tensions in such relationships.'

Des Crowley, Chief Executive, Bank of Ireland (UK)

'Rob Kendall is one of the world's leading experts on improving conversations. With *Workstorming*, he has applied his expertise to an area that sorely needs it: the workplace. Based on sound psychology, this is an absolute must-read for anyone wanting to communicate more effectively at work.'

Rob Archer, The Career Psychologist

'I was so glad to learn that Rob has written another book, and what a welcome addition it is to the art of good communication! In his usual clear style, and using an enjoyable and practical approach, Rob explains how to listen – truly listen – and teaches you how to convey exactly what you intend. This book is a treasure.'

Linda Blair, clinical psychologist, author, broadcaster and weekly columnist for the **Daily Telegraph**

WORK STORMING

Rob Kendall
The Conversation Expert

WORK STORMING

Why **conversations** at work go wrong, and **how to fix them**

W

WATKINS

Sharing Wisdom Since
1893

This edition first published in the UK and USA in 2016 by
Watkins, an imprint of Watkins Media Limited
19 Cecil Court
London WC2N 4EZ

enquiries@watkinspublishing.com

1 3 5 7 9 10 8 6 4 2

Typeset by Clare Thorpe

Printed in China

A CIP record for this book is available from the British Library

ISBN: 978-1-78028-917-5

www.watkinspublishing.com

CONTENTS

INTRODUCTION

Thinking back to your school days, which teacher do you owe a debt of gratitude to? In your working life, who has brought out the best in you? As a customer, when were you thrilled with the way a complaint was resolved? In each case someone was doing their job, but not in a business-as-usual way. If we were to examine what these people had in common, I'd wager that they excelled in speaking and listening.

Sadly, the converse is often true. We've all experienced teachers who extinguished our passion for a subject, colleagues who left us feeling downtrodden, and customer service that made us livid. These situations prove the same point: our success at work is inextricably linked to the way we communicate.

My first book, *Blamestorming* (2014), explores why conversations with our partners, children, parents, friends and work colleagues go wrong, and how to fix them. I introduced the 'warning lights' that indicate when a conversation's about to go off the rails. I examined why perfectly amenable interactions escalate into raging arguments, explained why the subtext of a conversation is often more important than what's being said, and outlined simple and practical steps to avoid misunderstanding. Although *Blamestorming* focused more on conversations at home than at work, it received encouraging reviews for its application in the workplace and was a finalist for Small Business Book of the Year. Even so, I felt I had only begun to explain the dynamics of communicating at work. I wanted to go deeper.

The result is *Workstorming*. As well as reintroducing the principles outlined in *Blamestorming*, this book examines the four coping strategies we use to deal with the sometimes overwhelming demands of the modern workplace: Stacking, Spinning, Skimming and Spilling. These strategies can damage your productivity, your relationships and your health, so *Workstorming* offers antidotes to boost your productivity, strengthen your connection with others and overcome information overload. It provides insight into the ways in which accountability, gender, culture, authority and power influence your conversations, and explains the key principles of negotiation, small talk, effective meetings and dealing with difficult individuals. And it describes how to avoid upset and confusion as you switch between face-to-face interactions, phone, email, online chat and text. Whatever your line of work, my aim is to equip you to have powerful and rewarding conversations in any circumstance at work, and with anyone.

For over 25 years, I've studied the best and the worst of communication. During a period of tectonic change, I've worked in more than 70 organizations across five continents, ranging from small start-ups to FTSE 100 companies, sports teams, government departments, charities and schools. I've seen organizations implode as a consequence of poor leadership and management, and witnessed others become billion-pound enterprises or create a legacy of social contribution. The transcripts that you'll read in *Workstorming* are mostly based on real situations and stories, and the recommended steps for action have been tried and tested in the fire of high-pressure working environments.

The title of this book reflects the dynamic nature of conversation in the workplace. The word *career* is a marvellous contradiction. It can either be a noun meaning 'an occupation with opportunities for progress' or a verb meaning 'to move swiftly and in an uncontrolled way'. Conversation can be characterized in much the same way. If our interactions were plotted on maps, they wouldn't be ruler-straight highways but mountain passes, full of bends and U-turns. If you want to improve your ability to navigate such terrain, *Workstorming* is for you. I look forward to hearing how you get on, and invite you to be in touch via www.conversationexpert.com.

Rob Kendall

Chapter 1

TAKE
Up the
CHALLENGE

HOW TO START TRANSFORMING YOUR CONVERSATIONS

To put it bluntly, conversations at work can be maddening. We desperately want to make a difference but our good intentions can be misread, our meetings can be wastefully unproductive and our best-laid plans can falter on the rocks of bureaucracy and disagreement. This is not to say that we don't have conversations that are uplifting, productive and inspiring, but why can't we have them more often?

When a conversation goes wrong we're naturally inclined to look for someone or something to blame but we can also be part of the problem. We've all experienced times when we knew what we wanted to say but couldn't find the right words, and we came away wondering what we *should* have said, or *shouldn't* have said, or where it went off track. But life offers minimal time for reflection, because our email inbox keeps filling up, our phone is constantly ringing and our to-do list demands our attention. An increasing number of us feel as if we're being hosed down each day with a deluge of information. When I ask people to describe their working day in a single word, the most common replies are 'exhausting', 'stressful' and 'relentless'. This has a profound effect on the way we interact with others. Stopping to listen becomes a luxury instead of a necessity, our interactions become more reactive, and we can end up having *mindless* rather than *mindful* conversations.

The problem is that our workplaces can only flourish if we communicate effectively. I once met a man who, when asked about his role, described himself as a 'professional meeting attender'; he felt the output of his interactions didn't remotely match the time and effort he invested in them. I've listened to similar frustration about poor communication in every enterprise that I've worked in, for the simple reason that they all involved people.

Thankfully, all is not lost – far from it. I hope that each of us has moments in our working life in which we feel heard, encouraged and collectively inspired to change the world, but how can we have more of those moments? In fact, how can we have them every day?

HOW WORK IS LINKED TO CONVERSATION

The *Oxford English Dictionary* defines conversation as: 'A talk, especially an informal one, between two or more people, in which news and ideas are exchanged.' For most of human history, talk required people to be within direct hearing distance, but that's all changed. The invention of the telephone is spectacularly modern in the context of 200,000 years of human history, and the period since the development of the worldwide web barely registers on the human time-chart, even though it's revolutionized the way we communicate. As long as it's a two-way exchange, talk can now be conducted face-to-face, via phone, email, online chat or text. For example, I treat two-way email correspondence in *Workstorming* as a conversation in which the person writing the email can be seen as the speaker and the person receiving it as the listener.

I've asked thousands of people what percentage of their average working day is taken up with conversation via one channel or another, and the answer is usually well above 50 per cent. If you're a teacher, or work in a customer-facing role or manage a team, you may say that it's closer to 90 per cent. Either way, your skill at speaking and listening will define your success. If you have a specialist technical job, conversation may not feature greatly in your working day. For example, artists in the visual-effects industry wear headphones and stare at computers in darkened rooms. But even they aren't sealed off from interacting with others; they need to clarify the scope of their work, raise problems with their producers and discuss their prospects for a pay rise. What's more, let's imagine that one of them is doing an excellent job and is asked to manage a team. The percentage of time she spends in conversation will transform overnight.

In short, conversation affects us all at work and the success of any enterprise is largely determined by the quality of our interactions.

WHY WE ALL NEED TO IMPROVE

If we accept that conversation plays a starring, or at least significant, role in our working life, it makes sense that an equivalent proportion of the school curriculum should be devoted to learning the principles, skills and practices of effective communication. But this isn't the case. Schools and universities offer few, if any, lessons in speaking and listening because it's assumed that we'll learn on a trial-and-error basis, in the same way that we learned how to walk.

Once at work, the situation is no different. Technical training tends to take precedence over training in conversation, so most of our learning happens on the job. We gain invaluable experience when we present our work to colleagues, lead difficult meetings or give tough feedback, but we ingrain bad habits too. It becomes normal to cut across each other's sentences, elbow our opinions into a conversation or zone out and disconnect from a debate. Just think of an average work meeting: how often do you feel like banging your head on the table? Afterwards you think to yourself, 'Was that really the best we can do?'

The answer is that we can all do much better. Despite studying the art, science and skills of conversation for more than two decades, I am continually challenged by the need to improve, and I desperately hope I'm never deluded enough to believe I've reached the summit.

FINDING MY VOICE

My own working life has been anything but mainstream. At the age of 18, I remember feeling quite lost. How on earth was I expected to know what career I wanted to follow? Having already lived on four continents during my childhood, I took the opportunity to escape such unsettling decisions by heading to India, where my introduction to working life involved supporting amputees who were being fitted with prosthetic limbs in a pioneering rehabilitation centre. These men came from humble communities across northern India, and most of them were recovering from horrific lorry crashes or railway accidents. It was self-evident that I, a shy and naive middle-class English teenager, couldn't begin to understand their language or their world and had nothing to contribute.

Stuck for an alternative, I discovered that drinking tea with them was a good place to start. And since I had little to say, I did my best to listen. As the days passed, the men told me their own stories through an interpreter, and I witnessed how the barriers of language and culture seemed to drop away. Encouraged by this, I put aside my embarrassment and drew portraits of them in my sketchbook. Since I had no more than school training, my drawings were average at best, but my willingness to look foolish seemed to bring us closer. Over time the generous hearts and gracious listening of these men gave me confidence that I could make a genuine contribution. In the most unlikely of circumstances, a world away from my own home, and in my first real job, I *found my voice*.

Returning to the UK, the reality of normal working life hit me hard. I did temporary jobs in a hospital laundry, a warehouse and selling art prints door-to-door. I went to university and emerged with a degree but didn't know what I wanted to do with it. I had no inkling that the next 28 years of my professional life would range from being a professional artist to co-launching a technology company, running a small-business consultancy, being a non-executive director for a BAFTA- and EMMY-winning visual-effects company and becoming an author. As a consultant, I've been fortunate to work with diverse teams across Europe, Asia, Africa,

Australia and the US. I've experienced the intensity of start-ups, the tensions implicit in joint ventures and the audacious challenge of delivering large projects such as the 2012 London Olympics. My roles have given me the opportunity to observe how people talk to each other, from the boardroom to the staff canteen.

Whether I've been working with a CEO who leads 50,000 staff or school leavers who are entering the workplace, I have asked the same question. Whatever your circumstances, and wherever you work, how do you find your voice and help other people to find theirs? Said in a different way, how can you communicate so that people become extraordinary around you?

This is where *Workstorming* comes in.

HOW THE BOOK WORKS

My aim is to support you as you go through the ups and downs of your working life. More specifically to help you:

- Prepare for difficult conversations so they're successful and rewarding.
- Respond mindfully to the unexpected twists and turns of conversation – disagreement, provocation, confrontation, confusion, difficult personalities and high-pressure moments – so you can keep your centre of gravity even if other people are losing theirs.
- Understand how to develop new ideas and opportunities through conversation, and turn them into effective action.
- Learn from the interactions that go well, and the ones that don't, and have the tools to recover a relationship when it seems to be broken. In this way, you can keep your conversations and your relationships healthy.

In each case, my gauge for an effective conversation is that it works for you *and* the person you're speaking to. No matter how well you think you've expressed yourself, other people will decide whether you were effective or not.

Each chapter in *Workstorming* focuses on a different aspect of communication that's relevant to you, whatever your role. I use examples and transcripts to illustrate how a conversation goes wrong and offer practical alternatives that would allow it go well. To this end, the book includes a cast of characters with a variety of challenges:

FINN works as a junior policy adviser for the government. He's fed up with his current role, and feels ignored by his boss **LIZZY**. His negotiation skills are tested as he looks for a new job.

HARRY is a serial entrepreneur, currently launching a new social-media app. He's brimming with ideas but can overreact and speak before he thinks, regretting it later.

JACK is regional manager for a sports-retail business. He rushes between conversations and doesn't make time to listen to his branch manager **OONA**, who needs to boost her sales figures.

LOIS is a member of the leadership team at a primary school. She loves teaching but she clashes with **MATT**, the school's head-teacher, because their communication styles are so different.

MARTHA works as a volunteer in the intensive-care unit of a hospital. Her day is filled with difficult conversations.

 MAYA is divisional head of marketing for a global consumer-products company. She struggles to find her voice in a highly male-dominated environment, leading to discussions with her manager, **LUKAS**.

 RAFA is an IT project manager for a financial-services company. He receives a crash course in understanding cultural differences when talking to **LIU WEI**, his counterpart in China.

 SAI is a construction manager, and partner to school teacher Lois. He feels torn between the demands of his authoritarian boss **KARL**, and staying true to his values.

 RIA is operations director for a telecoms company with responsibility for over 1,000 staff. She faces relentless demands on her time and gets a shock when her right-hand man **ALEX** says he wants to resign.

 ZOE owns a communications and live-events agency. Having built the business from scratch, she struggles to delegate to **ED**, who runs a key client account. She's married to entrepreneur Harry.

I trust that you'll see yourself in all the characters in *Workstorming* because their struggles are not specific to their role or industry. Each chapter will describe how their interactions can be more effective and fulfilling, and will conclude with a summary of recommended steps and a key lesson. I encourage you to read the whole book before returning to the chapters that are most useful to you.

DO YOU NOTICE ANYTHING?

Many years ago, I worked with a remarkable man who'd spent 20 years as a monk before getting married, starting a family and becoming a highly successful educator. I didn't see him regularly, but he was coming through London one day and had the afternoon free, so I took him to Hampton Court Palace.

I imagined that we'd go round the palace, but he seemed more interested in the garden, so we walked round that instead. I set out at my normal walking pace, which was almost a jog, but he wasn't in such a rush. He asked me when the blossoms came out, and although the same trees were in my street, I really couldn't remember because I always dashed past them. He enquired into the history of Hampton Court; I knew Henry VIII had lived there but couldn't remember anything else. He was aware that I'd been a professional artist and at one point he stopped to ask me about the correct name for a particular shade of red on one of the flowers. I said I had no idea.

I think he must have got a little exasperated at this point because he turned to me and said, in a gentle way, 'Do you notice *anything*?'

I'm not sure what I mumbled, but the following day I realized why I noticed so little. On my way to work, I was mulling over my to-do list. While reading my emails, I was thinking about getting on with proper work. During meetings I was pondering what I ought to be doing instead. My day continued like this, in a kind of blur, because I wasn't present to what I was actually doing. It seems that, half a millennium earlier, Leonardo da Vinci summed up my situation; it is claimed that he said, 'An average human looks without seeing, listens without hearing, touches without feeling, eats without tasting, moves without physical awareness, inhales without awareness of odour or fragrance, and talks without thinking.'

This issue isn't unique to me. A study by Harvard University psychologists concluded that people spend 46.9 per cent of their waking hours thinking about something other than what they're doing.[1] While this is a cognitive achievement in itself, it comes at a price: when our mind is wandering we are less happy, our relationships are shallower and our effectiveness diminishes. We can go through conversations in the same way – mindlessly.

WHAT TO DO?

STEP 1:
Start Noticing

When school teacher Lois starts paying attention to the dynamics of her conversations, this is what she discovers:

- She realizes that her speaking speeds up when she's disagreeing with a colleague. It's never really occurred to her before that she does this, but as soon as she recognizes the pattern, she's able to slow down her conversation and restore some balance to it.
- She notices how defensive she becomes whenever the parents of a pupil take issue with her teaching methods. By observing her response instead of justifying her actions, her emotions seem to loosen their grip on her.
- When she goes into her weekly staff meeting, she observes the dynamics of the interaction more closely than usual. She's always privately complained that her colleagues dominate the conversation by force of argument, rank or having too much

to say. But this time, she notices that she can also dominate the conversation by remaining silent.

When you place a higher value on noticing, you pick up the nuances and subtext of a conversation more easily, observe the impact of tone and body language more acutely and learn from every interaction, whether it goes well or goes awry. Instead of listening without hearing, and talking without thinking, conversations become richer and more fulfilling.

Lesson 1: Start to notice how little you notice.

Chapter 2

WATCH For the WARNING LIGHTS

HOW TO TELL WHEN A CONVERSATION'S GOING WRONG

It was 5:39pm on Monday 10 May 2010 and the political landscape in the UK was wide open. After 12 years of Labour government, the polls showed that the Conservative Party had won more votes in the general election than any other party, but not enough to gain an outright majority. Now the talk had switched to deal-brokering. Against this backdrop, Sky News was broadcasting from outside the Houses of Parliament in Westminster. Nothing was unusual about the opening scene in which Sky presenter Jeremy Thompson introduced Adam Boulton as Sky News political editor and Alastair Campbell as former director of communications for the Labour Party. But then a spectacular argument broke out on national TV between the two commentators. It was later described in the press as 'a remarkable and heated piece of footage from a remarkable day in politics'.[1]

Let's start with the bare facts:

- **Changes of speaker**: In less than seven minutes of conversation, there were 85 changes of speaker, of which 59 were mid-sentence interruptions.
- **Length of speech**: Boulton and Campbell each spoke for just 4.5 seconds on average before the other person cut in.
- **Speed of speech**: Normal speech runs at around 120 words per minute, but Boulton and Campbell accelerated to 278 words per minute when their argument reached its peak.

This situation is hardly unique; heated work meetings run along similar lines every day. We fall victim to a phenomenon that we could refer to as Right's Law, whereby we feel an irresistible urge to express our opinion even though the other person is neither listening nor interested in it, as Campbell and Boulton demonstrated during their encounter:

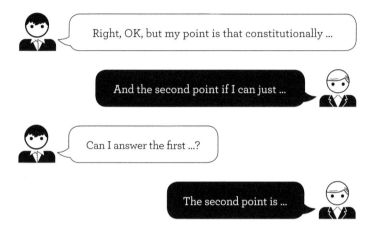

As their disagreement gathered pace, the language became more vivid and the accusations personal. Campbell claimed that Boulton had been saying for years that Prime Minister Gordon Brown was 'dead meat', while Boulton accused his counterpart of plotting. Their conversation reached a crescendo when Campbell said, 'You're obviously upset that David Cameron is not prime minister.'

I suspect that accusing a political commentator of lacking objectivity is the perfect way to get under their skin. It certainly worked on Boulton, who shouted, 'I'M FED UP WITH YOU TELLING ME WHAT I THINK!' Campbell, a battle-hardened political veteran, barely blinked as he forced home his advantage, saying: 'I don't care what you're fed up with, you can say what you like.' At last, with the air of a boxing referee who'd lost control of a fight, Jeremy Thompson stepped in to break things up. But it was a case of too little and too late.

We've all been in the same place as Boulton and Campbell, even if it wasn't on national television; there's nothing wrong with disagreement, challenge or even heated debate, which are the pillars of a healthy democracy. But life would be easier and more productive if we could spot the signs that a conversation is about to go wrong in time to change course. Perhaps this is the key to having mindful rather than mindless conversations. But it requires paying attention to the warning lights.

UNDERSTANDING THE WARNING SIGNS

Every day we rely on our gadgets to tell us when we're entering the red zone: think of the snooze button that warns you're oversleeping, or your car fuel indicator or the low-battery alert on your phone. But sometimes the warning lights are hard to spot, or we'd rather not heed them.

Nouriel Roubini is a financial analyst who predicted the market crash of 2007–8. A *New York Times* article described it this way: 'He laid out a bleak sequence of events: homeowners defaulting on mortgages, trillions of dollars of mortgage-backed securities unravelling worldwide and the global financial system shuddering to a halt.[2] Roubini was dismissed at the time as a crank, and afterwards people argued that he'd made a wild prediction that happened to come true, but he would say that he simply paid attention to the warning lights. Years on, he is still making the same point, urging the world to develop an early warning system for financial tsunamis.

On first impressions, the world of conversation may appear to be as unpredictable as the financial markets, but closer inspection proves that you *can* identify warning lights. The problem is that we don't know what they are, or we don't respond to them when we're in the heat of a difficult conversation, or both.

So how can you tell a meeting's starting to go off the rails, a client relationship is heading toward the rocks, or a conversation with your colleague is beginning to spiral? There are five warning lights you can watch for:

[1] Blamestorming – when the accusations and the criticisms are starting to fly and you're beginning to sound alarmingly self-righteous.

Blamestorming is a strategy for one-upmanship, in which we justify our own behaviour and assign fault to others. It's heavily driven by our emotions and is therefore very reactive. There are two ways in which this can play out:

- We'll criticize a third party when they're out of earshot while canvassing agreement for our own point of view. This is an easy game since the person in question isn't present. In doing so, we seek to take the moral high ground, knocking the other person down a peg or two and portraying ourselves as the innocent victim or the plucky hero. The more support we gather for our point of view, the more vindicated we feel in our opinion.
- The second form of Blamestorming happens face-to-face. Here it's a direct competition in which we fight to be right, using language such as 'you always' and 'you never' to bolster our argument. We're not interested in facts, or reflection, or in considering the other person's point of view.

How can you tell when you're Blamestorming? It's when you're more committed to finding fault than to resolving an issue.

[2] Escalation – when your emotions take over, inflaming your conversation to the point where logical thinking and rational discussion are thrown to the wind.

Unless you make efforts to defuse the situation, Blamestorming conversations can rapidly tip into Escalation. As one person's emotions rise, the other person's grow in equal or greater proportion, and a small-scale nuclear reaction occurs. When we escalate a conversation, our weaponry consists of accusations and justifications. Unsubstantiated claims and dirty tactics are the order of the day. When someone makes a particularly nasty accusation, we assume a look of surprise and innocence, as if we deserve to be a candidate for sainthood instead.

How can you tell when you're Escalating? You'll notice the intensity of an argument increasing fast, and the speed of the conversation will accelerate too.

[3] **Yes, But ...** – when you brush aside someone's opinions because they don't tally with yours, or dismiss their solutions because you don't feel heard.

Yes, But ... is usually a semi-polite way of dismissing what someone has just said and a form of objecting or blocking. More often than not it's used as a mid-sentence interjection; when one person says it, the other person will say it back, starting a ping-pong match of interruptions and diminishing listening.

How can you tell when you're in Yes, But ...? The short answer is that you'll hear yourself saying it, or the other person saying it. If this happens more than a couple of times, you'll know that neither of you is listening. The next time you go into a meeting where people have differences of opinion, notice how often you cut across each other's sentence with a Yes, But ...

[4] **Dominatricks** – when a conversation's flow and rhythm start to fall apart because you're trying to take control of it.

Being in Dominatricks doesn't necessarily mean that you're embroiled in an argument, but you'll be wrestling to take charge of the conversation or driving it toward your personal agenda, turning it into a battle of wills. As you do so, the natural rhythm of conversation will break down, and its coherence will begin to fragment.

How can you tell when you're in Dominatricks? The conversation feels competitive – you'll start to notice you're interrupting the person you're speaking with and not taking time to pause, listen and reflect.

[5] Mixed Messages – when you're speaking at cross-purposes or making assumptions without checking for mutual understanding.

Mixed Messages is not a trivial issue. One study estimated the cost to US and UK businesses at $37 billion per year. Of the 400 companies asked, 99 per cent reported that misunderstandings had put their company at risk of lowered sales and reduced customer satisfaction.[3] Given that we don't always manage to say what we mean, and often don't hear what other people say, every conversation has the potential for misunderstanding.

How can you tell when you're in Mixed Messages? There are two answers to this. The first is that you're not 100 per cent certain what's been said, or when an action needs to be delivered, or who's accountable. And the second is that you're not confident that others are on the same page as you.

WHAT TO DO?

STEP 1:
Pay Attention to the Signals

You may not be experiencing the fireworks of Escalation in your workplace, but you'll certainly be able to spot the other warning lights. Do Mixed Messages occur? How often do your meetings devolve into Yes, But ... exchanges in which you interrupt each other and forget to listen, rather than exploring each other's perspective? Do you or your colleagues practise Dominatricks in meetings, while others fold their arms and resign themselves to low-grade irritation? And do you engage in Blamestorming as a way of canvassing support for your point of view?

When we ignore the warning lights, we are likely to end up in one of the following places:

- **The Tangle** – where crossed wires lead to uncertainty and confusion, uncoordinated action and frustrated expectations.
- **The Big Argument** – where a conversation spirals into a bitter row with a work colleague, a supplier or even a customer.
- **The Bad Place** – where you're left feeling angry, upset or disconnected with someone after a conversation has gone wrong.
- **The Lock Down** – where someone withdraws from the relationship and is reluctant or unwilling to discuss it.

In truth we all get it wrong on a daily basis, and often little harm is done. But when this becomes the prevailing way that we communicate with each other, the cost in affinity and effectiveness starts to mount.

I have already extolled the virtue of noticing, and the same principle applies here. Rather than being quick to recognize and judge other people who ignore the warning lights, start to identify the signals in your own behaviour.

STEP 2:
Make a Choice

Having noticed the warning lights, you're still at liberty to say 'Yes, But ...', or to employ Dominatricks and Blamestorming, or even to engage in Escalation. It's your choice, but the difference is that you can choose consciously. Every time you see a warning light, you can press on regardless or you can change direction. And if you decide to press on, you can do so with open eyes.

Start noticing that conversations don't just happen. They are filled with choice points. At any moment, you can continue a conversation or stop it, speed it up or slow it down, maintain its rhythm or break it up. You'll only see the choice points if you pay attention to the underlying dynamics of the conversation rather than listening through your opinions. In theory this should be a relatively simple practice, but it seems hard to achieve, because the world appears to be spinning faster than ever. Either that, or *we're* the ones who are spinning faster.

Lesson 2: Respond consciously instead of reacting unconsciously.

Chapter 3

TAKE
Charge
AGAIN

HOW TO RECLAIM YOUR TIME AND YOUR SANITY

There's an old Zen story about a man and a horse. The horse came galloping through a village and its rider appeared to be rushing somewhere important. An onlooker called after him, 'Where are you going?' The rider looked over his shoulder and shouted, 'I don't know. Ask the horse.'

So often we can feel like the rider on the horse. Life seems to be taking us somewhere at tremendous speed – we're not altogether sure where – and we don't feel that we can stop. The horse is our calendar, or our demanding boss or our email inbox. We keep thinking that if we can grip tighter and stay in the saddle, the horse will – with luck, eventually, surely – slow down, allowing us to experience the scenery and the ride. But, just as we're about to get some breathing space, the horse gallops off again. We brace ourselves and cling on.

The problem comes when we reach the next village and find that the horse isn't slowing down. Our calendar is still crammed, our boss is demanding that we rise to a new challenge and our inbox is overflowing. So we keep riding. For many years, I thought that the solution to the problem was to ride faster. To save you the trouble of galloping for another 100 miles, I can vouch that this is a perfect recipe for a mindless life, because you don't ever get to live in the present. In my case, my work dominated our evenings and weekends. I didn't have the patience or reserves of energy to listen to my wife Sally, and I was too busy, exhausted or stressed to experience the moment-by-moment joy of being with our young children. It wasn't just the big moments that I was missing. It was the little moments, too.

There's a cartoon that perfectly expressed my situation, in which a man reaches the pearly gates of heaven and finds Saint Peter waiting at the entrance. Looking through his notes, Saint Peter says, 'Actually you had a pretty great life but you were looking down at your phone and missed it.' I kept saying to myself that things would get better and more manageable if I could hold on tighter or gallop faster but, privately, I knew that something had to give. Either I would burn out or I would fail in my job, or my relationships at home would be damaged. I'd always maintained that my family came first, but I was putting them second too often. And If I didn't make time for my children, why would they – later on in their lives – make time for me?

I knew that I wasn't alone in my predicament, because I've listened to thousands of people tell a similar story.

The problem was how to stop the horse. Further investigation led me to conclude that there's no single problem and no single solution. A series of forces contribute to the feeling that we're galloping faster and faster and, while these forces can offer incredible benefits to our health and our productivity, they bring downsides too.

EXPLOSION OF TECHNOLOGY

Our digital universe, which contains the data that we create and copy, is growing by 40 per cent a year, but the notion of having a connected world is in its infancy. The 'internet of things' is the new proliferation, referring to the number of devices that connect to the internet.[1] Today our phones and computers are connected to the web, but this will soon be the case for most of our household appliances too. The current figure of around 20 billion connected devices could increase to 50 trillion over the next 30 years.[2]

In 2045, robots are predicted to be as ubiquitous as computers are today. Apart from the obvious upside that they'll perform the tasks that we loathe doing ourselves, robots have the potential to hugely increase our quality of life and even save lives. For example, pioneering robots are being developed in Japan that can provide care for the elderly, an innovation driven by Japan's ageing population and shrinking workforce. Robots will also be used to perform many high-risk and high-skill activities, reducing the possibility of human error, and replacing us in the process. In the next three decades, robots may be able to conduct diagnoses of illness by travelling along the human bloodstream.

According to the Global Strategic Trends report, published by the Ministry of Defence in the UK, customer-service operations are likely to be enhanced to the point that a virtual telephone operator will be indistinguishable from a human one, thanks to advances in artificial intelligence.[3] While these innovations won't happen overnight, many of them are already on the horizon. Only time will tell whether we experience a corresponding deterioration in human communication skills.

INTERRUPTED WORK MODEL

In the late 1980s, my colleagues and I shared a single computer in our office, and it sat unattended for most of the day. My point is not about the march of technology but the fact that we were far less interrupted at work because we were less easy to contact. If I wasn't sitting at my desk, someone would leave a note for my return.

Now we can be reached at any time of the day or night so long as we care to turn our phones on. When company owner Zoe looks at her phone at midday, it displays three missed calls, two voicemail messages, two text messages, three Twitter notifications, eight Facebook messages and 182 unread emails. The temptation to check who's getting in touch is almost irresistible, and it doesn't help that her phone pings every time a new message arrives, with no consideration for whether she's in a meeting at work or putting her children to bed at home.

When Zoe sits in front of her computer, it alerts her each time a new email comes in and a banner briefly displays the sender of the message and its title. Like a siren call, this encourages her to stop what she's doing and check the contents. As the flow of messages accelerates, the gaps between interruptions become shorter. Researchers at the University of California tracked the average time people spent looking at a computer screen before switching their attention to another window. In 2004 the average time was three minutes. By 2012 this had dropped to one minute and 15 seconds and in 2014 it broke the one-minute barrier, averaging 59.5 seconds.[4] Our attention span is becoming gnat-like.

Part of the problem for Zoe is that she feels an obligation to reply to messages promptly. It's not that anyone's complaining about it, but responsiveness is a matter of personal pride for her. Once again, this characteristic is very common. In a survey of 1,100 people by the Institute of Psychology, more than half said that they always responded to an email 'immediately' or as soon as possible, with 21 per cent admitting they would interrupt a meeting to do so.[5]

The consequence of having so many interruptions is that tasks take longer to complete and contain more mistakes. A 2010 study by Workplace Options, an employee-support services organization, estimated that multitasking costs US businesses $650 billion a year in lost productivity through distractions.[6] This number is so big that I had to check if I'd made a typing error. It's hardly surprising that Zoe's conversations are reducing in length because she knows that, if she isn't quick, she will be interrupted again.

BLURRED BOUNDARIES

The fact that we can be reached wherever we are in the world means that we have to resist the temptation to dip back into work during our time off, but this isn't easy because the boundaries between our work and home life are becoming increasingly blurred. A study of employees in small- to medium-sized businesses across the US found that 81 per cent of workers check their work email at weekends, 55 per cent check email after 11pm and 59 per cent keep on top of their work email while on vacation.[7]

As Zoe and her partner Harry have highly demanding jobs, they recognize that urgent issues can spill into their evenings and weekends. This works up to a point, but can also cause bad feeling. Zoe often needs to make calls at unsociable hours, and Harry is currently preoccupied with negotiating a deal, prompting this conversation:

Sorry, I've got to work tonight or the deal might collapse.

You've been saying that for weeks.

Yeah, but they keep raising new questions on the contract. You can hardly talk – you always make calls in the evening.

Oh come on! Maybe once in a while, but your deal is round the clock. I've hardly seen you for a month.

As work spills into their home life, they are feeling the strain and having more Blamestorming and Yes, But ... conversations, leading them into the Big Argument and the Bad Place. Zoe would love to talk to Harry about her own stresses but doesn't want to burden him and instead feels resentful that his deal is having such a dominating influence. Harry also wants to offload but thinks he's better off keeping his problems to himself. Zoe and Harry's situation is perfectly normal, but this doesn't mean that it's healthy for their relationship.

PROLIFERATION OF INFORMATION

According to research conducted in 2014, business users send and receive on average 121 emails a day, and this is expected to grow to 140 emails a day by 2018.[8] The unchecked rise of the email culture reflects a wider picture in which we're absorbing more information and spending more time in front of screens. Our home life doesn't provide a sanctuary from information overload, either. The average media consumption for an adult in the USA has risen from 5.2 hours in 1945 to 9.8 hours today, thanks in large part to digital platforms streaming content via smartphones and tablets to wherever we are.[9]

This is a giant increase and perhaps it's inevitable that, while our exposure to information is constantly on the rise, the number of hours we're sleeping is declining. A third of adults in the UK sleep for between five and six hours per night, and almost half of them say that stress or worry keeps them awake at night.[10] It's no different in the US where fewer than half of adults under 50 think they're getting the sleep they need.[11]

While we have good reason to celebrate that we're living in the information age, it's also true to say that we're in the information-overload age.

HOW ARE WE COPING?

So how are we adapting to these challenges when we're at work? We have four principal coping strategies, each of which has an impact on how we conduct conversation. We could think of these as modern-day survival strategies:

[1] Stacking – the way we organize our *time*. Our tendency is to fill every available space in our already-bulging calendar so our commitments run back-to-back.

What's the impact of Stacking? You have no space to think, or tolerance for things to overrun, or time to deal with new issues as they emerge. If your diary is already full when you get to work, and further problems or opportunities come up that need your attention, you end up tagging them onto the end of your ever-lengthening day. Much as you value deeper conversations, Stacking doesn't encourage them. The poorer you are at declining demands on your time, the more likely you are to stack. In the process, you compromise your recovery time and become vulnerable to burnout.

[2] Spinning – the way we manage our *attention*. We run from one conversation to the next, frantically trying to keep up. By the time we get home we feel mentally scrambled, getting the illusion of speed but not necessarily the satisfaction of progress. When people ask how we are, we say that our head's in a spin.

What's the impact of Spinning? Just because you are physically moving from one conversation to the next, it doesn't mean you're mentally or emotionally engaged in them. As we have already seen, the more you spin, the more your attention span diminishes. Spinning lends itself to thinking errors, shallow conversations and loose ends.

[3] Skimming – the way we deal with the waves of *information* that crash over us. We skim to pick out the headlines and the urgent issues, and the focus is on speed rather than depth.

What's the impact of Skimming? Since the volume of information you consume has more than tripled since 1986 – equivalent to 175 newspapers a day – Skimming is an essential coping strategy for dealing with certain types of situation.[12] You can use it to scan your

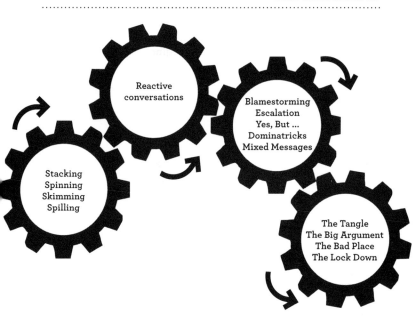

Twitter feed, catch the news headlines and check if your boss has sent you an email overnight. But if you skim when you're listening, you won't take the time to listen to the subtext or gather detailed information; Mixed Messages and poor decision-making are likely to follow. When you listen in this way, it leaves people with the experience that they're not getting heard, which in turn erodes the quality of your conversations and your relationships.

[4] **Spilling** – the way our *boundaries* get blurred. We're Spilling when we're reading our emails during a meeting, interrupting a one-to-one to take a phone call or checking who's sent a text message during a meal at home.

What's the impact of Spilling? People are left feeling that they don't have your attention or that they're being ignored. In their mind, they are playing second fiddle to your device, the demands of your boss or your schedule.

Your survival strategies do serve a purpose, helping you get through your working day. But, over time, their negative side effects will start to outweigh their short-term benefits. Like interlocking cogs, they increase the likelihood that you'll have reactive conversations, leading you into the Tangle, the Big Argument, the Bad Place and the Lock Down. While Stacking, Spinning, Skimming and Spilling are not inventions of the information age, their prevalence is a fundamentally modern phenomenon.

As operations director for a telecoms company, Ria lives away from home during the week. Because there's nothing to prevent her Stacking an evening meeting onto her working day or answering her emails at 5am, she sets a precedent of Spilling for her team members, who are keen to prove they can match her work rate but have to surrender their family time to do so. Family arguments ensue, causing stress that spills back into the workplace. Ria's feeling the strain too; after a week without any downtime, she's exhausted when she gets home for the weekend and has Blamestorming conversations with her partner.

THE STRESS FACTOR

Our foraging ancestors honed their ability to react almost instantaneously to threatening situations. This is known as a stress response and it's perfectly healthy when it's brief and acute, allowing us to escape from harm's way, but it's extremely unhealthy when it becomes prolonged and chronic. Think of the analogy of an elastic band: it can be extended to several times its length, but if you stretch it for long enough, it reaches a point where it won't spring back to its original size. If your body is in a continuous state of heightened alert, you'll find that you can't switch off even if you want to.

Chronic stress has damaging implications for our health and is becoming a major problem for employers, as these statistics show:

- In a study by the UK's Chartered Institute of Personal Development, 40 per cent of employers reported that stress-related absence has increased over the past year for their workforce. Just 10 per cent reported that stress-related absence has decreased.[13]
- According to the American Psychological Association, one-third of employees maintain chronic stress. Women report higher levels of work stress than men.[14]
- A survey conducted by Mind, a UK mental health charity, of over 2,000 individuals showed that 34 per cent of respondents considered their jobs very stressful, a higher proportion than those who blamed health issues (17 per cent) or money problems (30 per cent) for stress. The survey suggested that work is the number one cause of stress in people's lives.[15]

You may ask what stress has to do with conversation. Again, if you accept that you spend a significant proportion of your working day communicating with others, then it must be true that changing the way you conduct your conversations has the potential to reduce your stress levels.

WHAT TO DO?

STEP 1:
Take the Reins

While speaking to Sally one day about how to slow down my metaphorical Zen horse, I had a blinding realization. Rather than viewing the horse as the circumstances that were dominating my life, perhaps the horse represented my own habits. This gave me a different slant on the story. It was uncomfortable because I couldn't blame my habits on anybody else, but it was also liberating because they were my own habits, and so I could choose to change them.

Here are four antidotes to Stacking, Spinning, Skimming and Spilling that will allow you to start taking charge of your working behaviour again. Each of them replaces an existing habit with a new, more positive one:

- **Stacking antidote – create spaces in your day between commitments**: Schedule gaps in your day between meetings, in which you have nothing planned. Enter them into your calendar like any other commitment and use them for thinking time, or to have a conversation that's important but not urgent. Speak to a customer or supplier, catch up with a colleague in the hallway or discuss a long-term opportunity.
- **Spinning antidote – manage your attention**: You're not always going to give people your undivided attention, but you can notice when your attention drifts away during a conversation and then bring it back to the person you're speaking to. This is not a one-off process; it takes discipline and practice. Over time, you can turn the habit of being distracted into a habit of being present.
- **Skimming antidote – go deeper, not shallower**: Have fewer conversations, but take them deeper. Rather than Skimming so you can get on to the next task, take an extra minute to get clear, listen, think about the other person's perspective or check who's taking accountability. This way you'll reduce the chances of Mixed Messages and people will have the experience that you're listening to them rather than tolerating them.
- **Spilling antidote – put the boundaries back in**: Turn off your email during the evenings and weekends. There's very little that can't wait until tomorrow, and if someone urgently needs to reach you, they can call you and leave a message. The German employment ministry took the unprecedented step in 2013 of banning managers from emailing or calling staff outside working

hours, except in emergencies, so as to prevent burnout. A warning was clearly made that 'technology should not be allowed to control us and dominate our lives. We should control technology.'[16] If your company isn't so forward-looking, grasp the nettle yourself.

Each antidote will be explored in more detail throughout *Workstorming*. When I began practising them at work, I experienced an immediate uplift in my productivity and in the quality of my conversations. I was sufficiently encouraged to experiment with them at home. I turned off my emails and closed my computer for the weekend, only to discover that (God forbid) I wasn't indispensable after all. I found renewed time and energy to be the tickle monster and chase my kids up the stairs, or camp in the garden with them at the weekend. I was able to read them stories at bedtime without them going down to Sally and saying, 'Dad's fallen asleep in my bed again.' And mealtimes became a sacred space in which all devices were put away, and we talked instead.

As you take on regaining control, life's challenges won't go away. Depending on your job, your clients will continue to call and emails will stream into your inbox. You'll still need to juggle competing demands and commitments. But you don't need to wait for life to slow down before taking hold of the reins.

Lesson 3: Speed doesn't always lead to productivity.

Chapter 4

ENGAGE Your BRAIN

HOW TO BE MINDFUL, NOT MINDLESS

Entrepreneur Harry is feeling particularly stressed one morning. A falling-out with his wife Zoe before he left the house escalated into the Big Argument and now the train he's sitting on is delayed. As he skims through his emails, he finds one from his head of IT timed 23:42 the previous night:

> Harry, we've had a system outage tonight. The problem didn't come up in user-acceptance testing, so it's a new issue. The guys are working on it and we'll get it resolved ASAP. Joe

After barely a second's thought, Harry fires off this reply, in CAPITALS:

> JOE, I'M LOSING MY PATIENCE. THIS IS THE 2ND CRASH IN A MONTH. THERE WON'T BE A 3RD CHANCE!! WE NEED TO MEET!!

Scrolling further down his emails, Harry finds more updates from Joe. One was timed 01:15 and the other was timed 05:02. In them, Joe explains that he and two of his analysts were working at the office all night. They've identified the problem, which appears to be the responsibility of their third-party supplier, and have done a temporary fix before handing it over for further investigation today.

Harry immediately realizes that he's overshot the mark in his response. What's more, the IT guys who worked on the problem all night were copied in on Joe's email, and Harry pressed 'Reply all'. It won't have gone down well. He already lost a highly rated member of the technology team last week. When he asked her why she was leaving, she said she didn't like the working environment.

MINDLESS REACTIONS

Harry's explanation for his reaction is that 'he didn't think', but he says this to himself on a daily basis, and his emotional reactions can lead to the Lock Down, in which people withdraw from the relationship. If he can understand the difference between being mindless and being mindful, he can learn how to avoid needless friction. Mindlessness occurs when we get stuck in a narrow or fixed view of the world or react without thinking about our values or the wider context of a given situation. There are a number of different forms this can take, but here are two that are especially relevant to the way we conduct conversation:

[1] Emotional Triggers

Neuroscientist Dr Evian Gordon summarizes the overarching organizing principle of the brain as 'minimize danger and maximize reward'.[1] Without exception, any information received from your senses travels via your brain stem to your limbic system, where it's evaluated on the basis of whether it poses a threat or will help you survive. Broadly speaking, this area of your brain determines how you feel, allowing you to make decisions based on your emotions. It has no interest in your values, your long-term career prospects or the nuances of your relationships. It pays attention to what's directly in front of you, from one moment to the next.

If a threat is confirmed by your limbic system, even if it's on the basis of fleeting impressions, physiological processes are activated in preparation for a *fight*, *flight* or *freeze* response. Your pupils dilate, your heart rate increases and your body releases hormones such as adrenalin. To be clear, a threat doesn't have to relate to your physical survival; it can be a threat to your identity. For example, I asked my teenage daughters this question: 'If you're a passenger in a car with four friends and one of them is driving too fast, will you keep silent and hope for the best, or ask the driver to slow down?' Although we all know the right answer, it's a tough question because I'm asking them to choose between a potential threat to their physical survival and a threat to their reputation in front of their peers. Many teenagers, not to mention adults, may opt to put their identity first. For your limbic system, a threat is a threat, whatever the nature of it.

When you start looking out for examples of emotional reactions, you can see them everywhere. Barely a day passes without newspapers telling us how a comment, tweet or email has caused an uproar. Demands are made for heads to roll, apologies are usually forthcoming ('I apologise unreservedly for my lack of judgement ...'), and the next story breaks. Jeremy Clarkson captured worldwide headlines in 2015 when he punched a BBC producer after being told that he was too late to get a steak at his hotel. Of course it wasn't about the steak – it rarely is. When the story trickled out, it became apparent that he'd just had a cancer scare, followed by a long day of filming and several drinks. In our own workplaces, Stacking, Spinning, Skimming and Spilling create the perfect breeding ground for reactive behaviour.

During these moments, as we saw in the argument between Boulton and Campbell, we tend to:

- Jump to form judgements based on our emotions, rather than using facts and logic.
- Think in black-and-white terms, rather than in shades of grey.
- Take a catastrophic view on the situation, describing it as a 'disaster', or as 'carnage' or as an 'outrage', and look for something or someone to blame.

In Harry's case, his *fight* reflexes seem to be kicking in too often. It's not that he's swearing and shouting in the office, but he's certainly prone to mindless behaviour, and it's even worse with Zoe. If he barks, she reacts, and vice versa. Before they know it, they're in the Big Argument, the Bad Place or the Lock Down.

Let's not forget that emotional reactions aren't just about anger. Joe is sometimes quick to justify how a service problem isn't the fault of his technology team (*flight* response), but privately recognizes that they should have done much better. And primary-school teacher Lois is annoyed with herself that she didn't challenge a proposal in the department heads' meetings (*freeze* response). She stayed silent when headteacher Matt asked, 'Is everyone on board?', even though she totally disagreed with his idea. Now she's loath to backtrack and say she's unhappy.

[2] Autopilot and Mental Rules

It would be wrong to think that mindless behaviour is always connected to emotional reactions. Sometimes it's because you're applying a mental rule that you learned in the past without consideration for the current context. For example, I worked in a financial-services organization where a manager was delivering a new IT system and it preoccupied much of his thinking time. One day, he drove home from work and parked his car in his drive. As he got out of the car and started to walk toward his front door, he remembered that he no longer lived there. He'd moved three years earlier, but his mind was on autopilot and it had directed him to his old address. Feeling mortified, he drove off before he could be seen.

This might seem to be an extreme example, but we actually perform most of our daily tasks on autopilot. If you're an experienced driver, you arrive at your destination without any recollection of the journey, because the process of driving requires little conscious effort. If you're a competent typist, you can write an email without needing to look at the keys; your fingers somehow move to the right place on the keyboard. This principle extends into every aspect of your life, and there are extraordinary benefits to it, because you don't need to keep relearning the same tasks and your attention is freed up to focus on more important matters. But it can also lead to mistakes and mindlessness, because we're insensitive to changes in context and see what we expect to see. For example, every 45 seconds in the UK, someone fills up their car with the wrong fuel, even though the pumps are clearly marked and colour coded, creating an annual bill of £150 million per year for British motorists.[2] The worst months for this problem are March and September, when people have bought a new car and changed their fuel type. Like the manager who went to his previous address, they apply the old mental rule to the new situation, making an expensive error.

Our mental rules are mostly invisible to us. For instance, you may get very anxious if you wander into a field wearing a red shirt and see a bull. In this case, you'll apply the mental rule that you've learned from photos of matadors waving red flags. But bulls are colour blind, and therefore the colour of your shirt is irrelevant. It's the motion of material that provokes their fight response, so you'll be most vulnerable to attack if you're wearing a long scarf or a billowy dress. If you didn't know this fact already, I have just reset your mental rule. Now imagine that you have thousands of mental rules about yourself, your profession and the colleagues you work with. They shape your thinking and determine your view of the world. Most of the time they may work perfectly well for you, but they can also lead you to see something that isn't there, or fail to see something that is there.

A few years ago, a colleague and I ran a leadership programme in an organization in which we asked the participants to build a structure in the fastest possible time, competing in teams against their peers. Many of them were brilliantly accomplished engineers. Nevertheless, because they were attempting the task for the first time, it was difficult for them to figure out the optimal sequence in which to assemble the components and they lost time as they tried different configurations. Of course, the real experts in the room were my colleague and I, simply because we'd seen the structure built dozens of times and had learned all the pitfalls. Nobody in the room thought to ask us the best way to go about it, even though we added a note at the bottom of the instructions saying, 'You can ask us any questions that will help you accomplish your task', and we repeated this instruction verbally. We ran the programme over 50 times on three continents, meaning that around 1,000 leaders participated, and not once did it occur to anyone to ask us how to construct it, because they assumed this would be against the rules. If asked, we'd have willingly told them. The consequences of this are significant for any organization wanting to create a culture of innovation.

MINDFUL RESPONSES

The real question is how we can develop mindful responses, and there are three principal elements to this:

[1] You need to **notice your own thoughts and feelings**. Since you don't choose them, you can't switch them on and off like your radio or your cooker, but you can choose how you respond to them. Harry is a good case in point; when he emails Joe, he allows his irritation and anger to determine his behaviour.

The solution is not for him to eradicate his feelings but for him to notice his feelings and then – independently of them – to *choose* his response. If he can make this distinction each time he experiences strong emotions or negative thoughts, he can feel irritated and yet respond in a way that isn't governed by his irritation. This would be liberating for Harry because he often feels at the mercy of his negative emotions.

[2] You need to **be open to new information and alternative perspectives**. Harry doesn't think to check for further information before sending his email, because he has a single view in his mind that Joe and his team have messed up again. Once he has the wider context from Joe's subsequent emails, his reaction suddenly seems inappropriate and – well – mindless. When interacting with someone else, being mindful requires consideration for the other person's context, and this is where listening comes in. You can say the same thing to two different people, and later reflect that it was mindful in one instance and mindless in the other.

[3] You need to be able to **reference your own commitments and values**, since these become your compass in a mindful conversation. By not speaking up in the leadership team meeting, Lois received a temporary emotional reward – avoiding embarrassment – but she's created a bigger issue that she hadn't considered in the heat of the moment. Now she needs to go along with an idea that she disagrees with or has to tell her boss that she doesn't support his proposal after all. If she can reference her values in these difficult situations, she's more likely to find her voice and give a mindful response.

WHAT TO DO?

STEP 1:
Get Your Rational Brain Involved

Let's say that you believe you're at home on your own, and don't hear your partner come through the door. When he or she comes round a corner, your limbic system sounds the alarm and you physically jump and perhaps shout for good measure. When you recognize your partner and reach a logical explanation for their appearance, you admonish them for frightening the life out of you. A false alarm has now been declared and your heart rate begins to calm down. In this situation, the emotional reaction and the logical explanation are happening in different parts of your brain, but the emotional reaction always comes first. For this reason, the old adage of taking a deep breath is sound advice, because it allows your rational brain to catch up.

The limbic system is often referred to as the 'old brain' because it shares characteristics with our ancient ancestors and mammalian cousins such as chimpanzees. In contrast, the pre-frontal cortex is the most recent addition to the brain system and is uniquely human. It allows you to consider the facts, see shades of grey and think about the longer-term implications of an action. But it takes effort to use it, and you need to consciously activate it. If you ride your emotional wave, as Harry did when he fired off his email, and don't get your rational brain involved, you may regret it down the line when you have more information.

When you operate on autopilot, you're drawing on the areas of your brain associated with habits and the retrieval of memories. The application of a mental rule occurs so quickly and automatically that you don't even notice it's happening. Perhaps it's more accurate to say that the rule thinks you. This works perfectly well much of the time, except when it doesn't. We've already seen how you can get caught out if you apply the rule without considering the nuances of the current context or assimilating new information, and the odds of this happening are greatly increased when you're Spinning and Skimming.

If we rerun Harry's scenario on the basis of engaging his rational brain, his thought process might go as follows:

- He would start by noticing his emotional reaction and then check for new information, seeing if Joe had sent any messages after 23:42 the previous night.
- Having found Joe's subsequent emails and logged that the IT guys had probably been in the office all night, Harry would identify his values and conclude that now isn't the time to give them a rocket. Besides, email would be the wrong channel for delivering it. The logical approach would be to clarify the facts and root causes of the problem with Joe, before agreeing a joint way forward.
- Finally, Harry would consider the best action to take right now. He could either leave the whole situation until he reaches the office in half an hour, or send a holding email. In the end, he decides to send a reply as follows, copying in the analysts who worked overnight:

> Sounds like you've been in the office all night, so thanks to all 3 of you for your efforts. It's worrying to have another system crash, even though you've got a fix in place. Joe, let's chat later today when you've had some sleep, and decide what's next. I'll check my diary when I get in and clear some time.

I'm not saying that involving your rational brain gives the right answer every time, but it allows you to think through the options and reference them against your values and commitments before taking action. Just as you can't see your reflection in boiling water, so you can't always see a situation clearly when your emotions are raging.

STEP 2:
Restore the Pauses

Try reading this piece of text:

> In a sentence punctuation marks such as commas full stops and brackets are used to separate sentences and elements they allow you to navigate successfully through the text and clarify meaning the gaps are as important as the words creating spaces in between commitments and conversations works in much the same way you ignore them at your peril

Now try it again:

> In a sentence, punctuation marks such as commas, full stops and brackets are used to separate sentences and elements. They allow you to navigate successfully through the text and clarify meaning. The gaps are as important as the words. Creating spaces in between commitments and conversations works in much the same way. You ignore them at your peril.

The commas and full stops are pauses that help you create meaning. As Mark Twain once said, no word was ever as effective as a rightly timed pause. When you stack your conversations, they lose their coherence.

Reclaim the punctuation marks in your day instead of letting them get squeezed out, and use these moments to engage your rational brain, reflect on your values and decide the best way forward. A study by the Draugiem Group found that their employees who had the highest productivity didn't put in the longest hours; instead, they took regular breaks. On average, they took 17-minute breaks for every 52 minutes of work.[3] When you're caught up in your coping strategies of Stacking, Spinning, Skimming and Spilling, it will feel as if you don't have a moment to lose and must push on. At these times it's worth remembering the old Zen saying: 'Meditate for 20 minutes a day, unless you are too busy, in which case meditate for an hour.'

STEP 3:
Choose Your Channel

When you speak to someone face-to-face, you use a rich variety of cues to piece together what they mean. You register their tone of voice, how they lift their eyebrows, where they pause and whether they make eye contact with you. Much of this is happening without any conscious awareness on your part. But when you're having an email conversation, all you have is the words, so the likelihood of getting into the Tangle is greatly increased.

The different types of communication typically used in the workplace, and the benefits each of these offer (or don't offer), are summarized in the table opposite.

When it comes to expressing feelings, we can use emojis to help us get around the limitations of text and email. For example, I can cut a long story short by sending you this:

Writer's block today. Aagghh!!! 😬😔🤓😟😫

Some people would say that they find it easier to express feelings via email or text than face-to-face. But as a general principle in the workplace, email and text are best used for transferring information,

BENEFITS

TYPE OF COMMUNICATION	Full set of visual clues	See body language	Hear tone	Express feelings	Convey information
Face-to-face	✓	✓	✓	✓	✓
Video	✗	✓	✓	✓	✓
Phone	✗	✗	✓	✓	✓
Email	✗	✗	✗	✓	✓
Instant message and text	✗	✗	✗	✓	✓

such as confirming the time of a meeting, distributing the pre-reading materials for it, or forwarding the minutes afterwards. For tricky conversations, the chances of feeling misunderstood or offended are greatly increased if you don't have visual and auditory cues. For example, Joe emails Harry and asks him to approve a purchase order for software licences and new hardware. He doesn't hear back for 48 hours and, when he sends a reminder, Harry replies like this:

If we must.

If Harry had spoken these words, Joe would have realized that his boss was saying 'yes' in a lighthearted and sardonic way. Instead, Joe is irritated and he stews on Harry's email all evening. In his mind, it's one more piece of evidence that Harry is rude and dismissive. Perhaps most important of all, he's not certain whether Harry has given his approval or not, because the 'yes' is inferred.

There are two lessons from this:

- Bearing in mind the potential for ambiguity, make extra efforts to explain your context when communicating by email or text.
- As a general rule, never tackle an issue by text or email. The fact that email is easier, and avoids a face-to-face conversation, doesn't mean that it's right. If you want to resolve a conversation that's going wrong, move as far *up* the communication chain as you can, switching to a channel that allows you hear the other person's tone of voice or, better still, see their body language.

But the first job is to think before you act.

Lesson 4: The busier you are, the more pauses you need.

Chapter 5

LISTEN
Before
SPEAKING

WHY LISTENING COMES FIRST, AND SPEAKING SECOND

In an article for the *New York Times*, the author Henning Mankell commented on the fact that, when doing TV interviews in the Western world, he has to answer a question so much more quickly than he did a decade ago, and he remarked that people seem to have lost the ability to listen. Mankell contrasted this with his experience in Africa, where people find the time to listen slowly and the art of storytelling doesn't have to follow a direct path to a conclusion.[1] People often tell stories in parallel, skipping between them, and eventually coming back to tie the threads together. This would be far too indirect and long-winded for our Western way of listening.

Mankell recounts a day in Mozambique when he sought respite from the suffocating heat by sitting on a stone bench where two old men were already seated. One of the men was recounting how he'd visited a third old man, who began to tell him an amazing story about his life. As night fell, they decided to pause the story and reconvene the following day. But on his return, the visitor found the old man had died. The listener on the stone bench fell silent, before finally saying, 'That's not a good way to die – before you've told the end of your story.'

Mankell's message is about the difference between slow listening and fast listening. He reminds us that our ability to listen makes us uniquely human: 'What differentiates us from animals is the fact that we can listen to other people's dreams, fears, joys, sorrows, desires and defeats – and they in turn can listen to ours.'

So here are two ends of the spectrum on listening. At the fast end, we are rushed and distracted. Rather than listening, we are preparing to speak. We skim people's sentences, pick out the gist of what they're saying, and then pitch in with our opinions and solutions. At the slow end of listening, we hear people out. By giving them our attention, we allow them to be heard and give them space to think. In doing so, we celebrate our humanity and create reservoirs of trust.

It seems obvious that we should aim for the slow end of the listening scale, but what are the implications for delivering our accountabilities and meeting our objectives? And, even if we believe it's the right thing to do, how on earth do we find the time?

LISTEN SLOWLY

Jack is regional manager for a retail business and has 12 branch managers who report to him. Ideally he would have fewer direct reports, but times are tough and resources are stretched. As he spins and skims to keep up, his stress levels are high and his attention span is short.

Jack's work habits have started to spill into his home life. Last night he asked his six-year-old daughter Ellie about her day but, in truth, he was too distracted to listen. Noticing that she was speaking very fast, Jack asked her to talk more slowly. Ellie looked him in the eye and said: 'Then listen slowly!' He was quite shaken by her reply; she had fired an arrow directly to the heart of the problem, as only children can, but he had no idea how to solve it.

Now he's having a bad day – good days are few and far between at the moment – and he's Spinning even more than usual when he gets a call from Oona, one of his store managers. The moment Jack picks up the phone, he thinks he should have let it go to voicemail. 'I'll make it super-quick,' he says to himself, 'just as long as it isn't about a staffing issue.' It starts like this:

Jack, have you got a moment?

Er … yeah … if it's quick. What do you need?

It's a staffing issue.

CONVERSATION, NOT NONVERSATION

Jack and Oona are about to have a *nonversation* rather than a *conversation*. Jack isn't listening, and here are the reasons:

[1] **His listening is biased** – when we listen through our biases, we pull past-based conclusions into the current conversation and listen through them. In doing so, we tend to look for evidence to support a conclusion rather than evidence to disprove it. This is known as a *confirmation bias*. Jack has concluded that Oona is *always* raising staffing issues and he gets irritated when the topic comes up. For her part, Oona has noticed that whenever they talk about a staffing problem, she feels as if she's being blamed, even though staff turnover in the branch was higher under her predecessor. The conversation is over as soon as it's begun, because Jack is consolidating his pre-existing point of view instead of listening.

[2] **The set-up is all wrong** – even though Oona asks Jack if he has 'a moment', she knows the conversation will take longer. She's worried that if she asks for 15 minutes, he'll say he doesn't have time and their conversation will be delayed. As for Jack, he's rushing between meetings and doesn't really have time to talk, but he takes the call now because he knows his diary is stacked all day. Neither of them is fully *in* the conversation, or fully *out* of it, because the set-up is wrong.

[3] Jack is listening 'quickly' – he wants Oona to get directly to the point. All the branch managers – and Jack's six-year old daughter Ellie – know that they have to speak quickly because Jack will listen quickly. Conscious of this, Oona tries to cram too much information into a few sentences:

Sorry Oona, it's not a great time right now;
just give me the bottom line.

OK, thanks. I've got a staffing problem and need some help. One of my staff – Maria – is off sick with stress. I don't know when she's going to come back because ... long story short ... her son's ill. Then I've got Ben ... if you remember, you were impressed with him when you last did a store visit ... anyway, he wants to move from a fixed contract to casual employment. This means I'm short of permanent staff ...

Sensing that Jack is distracted and doesn't have time to listen, Oona trades coherence for speed and scrambles her sentences.

[4] Jack is distracted and disengaged – while Oona is speaking, Jack is checking his emails to see where his next meeting is. He skims what she's saying and, after catching the gist that she's short on permanent staff, he cuts in:

Oona, sorry to interrupt. I know this staffing issue is an ongoing saga, but I've got to run now. Can I give you a call tomorrow? I'll see if I can reach you when I've got 10 minutes free.

Fine. Speak to you then.

But Oona isn't fine with the outcome because Jack sounded dismissive and she's offended by his reference to her staffing issue as an 'ongoing saga'. Meanwhile Jack moves on with his day. It crosses his mind that he's done to Oona exactly what he did to his daughter Ellie last night. But, because his diary is stacked, he has to keep Spinning and there's no time for further reflection.

BEING PRESENT DOESN'T TAKE LONGER

Nobel Peace Prize winner Malala Yousafzai was shot by the Taliban for going to school. In an interview with World Bank Group president Jim Yong Kim, she described how she knew that she was in grave danger. She prepared herself for the moment a Talib would come to shoot her, describing it this way: 'I will tell him, "Shoot me, but listen to me first. Listen to my voice. Listen to what I say.'''[2] It's extraordinary to think that she was willing to trade her life to be heard. In doing so, she gave listening a value beyond measure. If only we could give listening a fraction of this value in our work.

The idea that we don't have time to listen is mostly an excuse. Listening starts with being fully present in the conversation that you're in. This doesn't necessarily increase the length of your interactions; it can make them shorter. When we give people our full attention, they feel that their speaking has value because they are being heard. The evidence to support this claim is irrefutable. From 30 years of behavioural economic research by Gallup, involving over 25 million employees, it is clear that one of the key predictors of employee engagement is whether people feel their opinions count.[3]

When I work in organizations, I ask people to tell me their own listening highlights. One manager, Martin, recalled the time his construction firm renovated the Royal Academy of Dramatic Art in London. Sir Richard Attenborough was RADA's president and Martin's firm invited him to their Christmas party, without the slightest expectation that he would turn up. As they celebrated in a London pub, the great man came in unannounced to thank them for their work. For the duration of their conversation, Attenborough was utterly engaged in Martin's world. There was no sense that he was just going through the motions, preparing to speak or wanting to rush home. He listened slowly and chose to be nowhere else, before moving to the next person and doing exactly the same with her.

Hospital volunteer Martha also listens in this way, and she does it every day. She works in a hospital intensive-care unit, and family members who visit the ward are in a high state of stress and anxiety. Not only does she greet them when they arrive, but she makes sure she's alongside them when a consultant has delivered heartbreaking news. She can't change the harsh reality of their situation but she doesn't underestimate the power of listening slowly in the moment when they need it most. Few of them ever forget her contribution.

WHAT TO DO?

STEP 1:
Practise Being In the Conversation You're In

If you're a manager and persist in listening quickly, people won't raise their challenges, concerns and questions with you, and you'll only know they're unhappy when they hand in their resignation letter. The same is true at home. As she grows up, Ellie will stop talking to Jack if she thinks he's too preoccupied with Spinning and Skimming to hear her out.

The solution is to take on being present in each and every conversation. You're never going to accomplish this all the time but it's something to strive for. If you don't manage it in this conversation, the next one is always round the corner. Since we're all starting from such a low base, even a 10 per cent improvement will have knock-on benefits for your productivity and relationships.

While Jack is speaking to Oona, his mind chatter interferes incessantly, and it goes like this:

> I haven't got time for this conversation ...
> Here she goes again ... More staff issues ...
> I shouldn't have answered her call ... Where's my
> next meeting? ... I've think the location's on the
> email invite ... Now I'm late ... I need to have this
> conversation another time ...

Your thoughts and feelings are never going to disappear altogether, so the best option is to notice them and keep bringing your attention back to the conversation you're in, before the process repeats itself. Each time you mentally drift away, return your attention to the conversation again. Over a period of time, this will start to become a habit. As you become more present, your affinity with people will deepen and your productivity can only go up.

STEP 2:
Consciously Shift Between Conversations

Let's say you're in the middle of some work at your desk when a colleague appears and asks for a quick chat. There are two ways you can deal with this. You can either say that you're in the middle of something and offer to speak to them in half an hour when you can listen properly, or you can stop what you're doing and have the conversation now. If you decide to speak now, the challenge is how to shift your attention.

The following visualization will help. Imagine that you are turning *off* a switch that relates to the task you were doing a moment ago. In doing so, you're mentally and emotionally letting go of that task, at least for a minute or two. Now imagine turning *on* a switch that relates to the person in front of you. You are developing a new mental prompt, reminding you to bring your mind as well as your physical presence to the new conversation. In this way, you prevent Spilling by strengthening the boundaries between each task.

Given that you'll shift your attention hundreds of times each day, your effectiveness will be transformed if you can switch on and switch off between tasks. You can even practise this as you read your emails by taking the view that each message is a different conversation. As you open a message, you switch on, and as you finish replying or delete it, you switch off. If Jack can practise this regularly, it won't go unnoticed by Oona and Ellie. When they're with him, they'll feel that they are having conversations instead of nonversations.

Lesson 5: Remember that 'silent' is an anagram of 'listen'.

Chapter 6

MAKE
Your meetings
COUNT

HOW TO GET MORE WORK DONE IN LESS TIME

We all come up with ways to counter the tedium of bad meetings. I remember one business where the CEO had called together 40 leaders for a two-day strategy meeting with external consultants. To lighten up a slow session, everyone played the old game of passing each other a word or sentence to say without the consultants or the CEO noticing. It started with references to 'low-hanging fruit' and 'getting our ducks in a row'. Predictably enough, the challenges became more obscure. Things reached a peak at the start of the second day when the consultants were outlining the agenda and someone asked if he could make a point. Welcoming such enthusiasm first thing in the morning, he was ushered to the front. 'I'd like to give some feedback from yesterday,' he said in a deadpan voice. 'I thought it was supercalifragilisticexpialidocious.' We rolled with laughter like eight-year-olds.

Looking back, perhaps my tedious lessons at school were intended to be preparation for meetings at work. A Dilbert cartoon sums up the problem well. The office boss asks Carol, his secretary, to schedule a meeting. When she asks what the topic of the meeting is, he replies, 'I plan to fuse six sigma with lean methods to eliminate the gap between our strategy and objectives.' Without so much as a sideways glance, Carol replies, 'I'll just say "waste of time."'

According to TED speakers David Grady and Jason Fried, the average executive attends 62 meetings a month, but over a third of these are considered to be unnecessary or a waste of time. Given that executives spend 40–50 per cent of their time in meetings, this means they're wasting over two months a year. Grady and Fried go on to say that the bill for poor meetings is $37 billion a year in the US alone.[1] Bad meetings steal time and money.

Research shows that, on average, 15 per cent of an organization's collective time is spent in meetings and this figure is increasing year on year. One study, published in the *Harvard Business Review*, estimated the amount of time people spent supporting *one* weekly executive meeting in a large organization, based on analysing the Outlook calendars of their employees. It concluded that a whopping 300,000 hours a year were spent supporting that single meeting, taking into account the downstream cascade of team meetings that fed into it.[2] Astonishingly, this figure only included meeting time, and excluded additional preparation.

Since meetings are conversations, how we can reverse the trend?

WORK BACKWARD NOT FORWARD

Let's start with the four words, 'Let's have a meeting'. They seem innocent enough, but they probably cause more problems and waste more time than any other sentence in the workplace. Rather than questioning whether a meeting is necessary, the normal response is, 'Good idea. When do we want it, and who should we invite?'

Now that a vague intention ('let's meet') and a broad topic (such as 'project review') have been established, calendars are opened and dates and names suggested. Someone says, 'I think we should get a representative from marketing', and another says, 'Yeah, well in that case we probably need a person from finance.' Finally, after settling on a date and a venue, someone says, 'Shall we stick it in for an hour?' and calendar invites are sent out. When your meeting does eventually take place, a curious and amazing thing happens: it lasts for exactly an hour. This is because the conversation expands, like a giant sponge in water, to fill the allocated time.

This scene is so normal, and gets re-enacted so many times each day, that it barely provokes a flicker of outrage, but it is almost criminal in nature. To transform your meeting culture, make sure that three questions are asked *before* invites are sent out:

[1] **What's the purpose of the meeting?** This clarifies the reason for having it.

[2] **What are the intended outcomes?** This answers what you want to come away with.

[3] **Whose meeting is it?** This tells you who's accountable for it.

Answering these questions requires you to fire up your rational brain. Once you've done so, you can *think backward* from your purpose and intended outcomes to figure out who needs to be there, how much time is required, whether you can conduct the meeting by conference call or face-to-face, and where it will be held. And the person who's accountable for the meeting can decide who needs to attend. This is a totally different thinking framework to one in which you *think forward* toward a vague intention.

I've never met a great leader or manager who doesn't follow this process of working backward from the outcomes they are committed to. For example, Sir Dave Brailsford was performance director for the GB cycling team from 2003 to 2014. After a century of underperformance, British cyclists won 10 Olympic gold medals and 59 world championships during his tenure. Now at Team Sky, and seeking to win the Tour de France each year, it's no surprise that Brailsford describes his role in this way:

> *My job is to look at the best probabilities to try to win, to picture someone on that podium with the yellow jersey, on the Champs Elysée, and work back from there.[3]*

First get clear on purpose and outcomes, and then figure out how to make them happen. You can practise this approach in relation to any endeavour or project, and doing so for meetings is a good place to start. After a while, it becomes a way of life.

Once you're clear on the outcome, a new question arises. What type of meeting do you need to have?

WHAT KIND OF MEETING IS IT?

A meeting in which you're creating a 10-year vision for your organization with 50 of your leaders is quite different from one in which you're seeking to win new business with a client, or one in which you need to give difficult feedback to a moody colleague. We cannot apply a one-size-fits-all approach and therefore need to be adaptable. There are dozens of different meeting types, but here are four that will come up time and again:

[1] Operational Meetings

- **What's going wrong?** Company owner Zoe's weekly operational meetings last nearly two hours and have turned into a battle of Dominatricks and Yes, But ... conversations. She's tried making it a tightly structured conversation, with a similar format each time, but this felt too rigid and each topic became protracted. Then she made it more free-flowing, but the meeting has become a talking shop. Its purpose has become hazy and her team members only attend because it's in their diaries.
- **How to fix it?** Zoe resets the purpose and intentions as follows: to raise issues and opportunities on key projects, and to agree priorities for the coming week and month. Other issues can either be dealt with on an individual basis or put on the agenda for their half-day monthly meeting. By resetting their aims, a new sense of energy and momentum is created and they find they can finish in 50 minutes. To ring the changes, they also occasionally follow Richard Branson's advice and have stand-up meetings.

[2] Meetings for Decisions

- **What's going wrong?** Rafa's company has outsourced its administration services to a third-party supplier, which has in turn passed on the development work for the new IT release, creating a long delivery chain. Rafa sets up a three-way meeting to agree the launch date for the new release, but it devolves into a bitter disagreement. Is it a joint decision by all three parties? Or is it Rafa's? Or is it really a decision for Rafa's boss? None of them knows who's accountable for the decision.

- **How to fix it?** Before going into a meeting where a decision needs to be made, Rafa has to be crystal clear who the decision-maker is. Literally stated, the word 'decide' means to 'cut off the alternative', but if you don't know who's making the choice, it's like a tennis match where it's not clear if the umpire, the players or the spectators are going to make the line calls. If it's agreed that Rafa is accountable, then he needs to clarify how the decision process will work. Here are his choices:

  - *Make a unilateral decision.* If he's already made up his mind, it's best to be honest about it, so that he doesn't waste everyone's time.
  - *Make a decision after input.* It's perfectly legitimate for Rafa to hear differences of opinion around the table and then make the call, given that he's accountable for the decision.
  - *Take a majority vote.* If he goes down this route, Rafa must be clear in his own mind that he'll accept the group's decision even if it opposes his own.
  - *Look for a full consensus.* By opting for this strategy, Rafa must consider what he's going to do if there's a split decision.

Rafa can't flip-flop between these. If he clarifies how the process will work up-front, and sticks to it, he will avoid the Tangle.

Lastly, Rafa must be clear in his own mind on the timeframe in which the decision needs to be made. Does it have to be today, or can he buy another 48 hours to validate assumptions before committing to a launch date? Knowing the answer to this will have a strong bearing on the conversation.

[3] Meetings to Create New Ideas

- **What's going wrong?** Entrepreneur Harry has a dozen new ideas a day and frequently throws them into his meetings, to the bewilderment of his team members, who think he's like a missile that constantly veers off-course. Harry believes his ideas are always received negatively, and this irritates him because he is – after all – the founder, CEO and majority shareholder of the company. In their defence, his team members are trying to be the voice of reason. They'll have to implement Harry's ideas and feel obliged to point out the practical implications at the outset, thereby saving time, money and effort down the line. They end up in Yes, But … conversations, which annoys Harry. He complains to Zoe when he gets home, and his team members moan to each other when he's out of earshot.
- **How to fix it?** Harry is giving Mixed Messages and the problem could be solved if he communicated more clearly what he wants from his team. Let's consider this question, asked by Harry in a team meeting:

What about doing a deal with a content provider?

Harry's team members don't know how to react. Is this a throwaway comment? Does he want their opinions now about whether it's a good or bad idea? Or is he suggesting that someone looks into it later? He can make things easier by rephrasing his question:

> This is not for discussion now, but I wonder if we can do a deal with a content provider? Can we dedicate some time to this at our next meeting?

When they do discuss Harry's suggestion, he needs to tell them how he wants them to participate:

> Let's take 20 minutes to explore the idea of doing a deal with a content provider. This is a speculative conversation. I'm not going to hold you to anything, so please put aside the reasons why it can't be done, and don't kill off each other's ideas. What's the opportunity?

Rather than constraining them, Harry gives his team members more freedom to think creatively by putting clear signposts and boundaries around the conversation. When he does so, he may be surprised at their contributions.

[4] Meetings to Resolve Issues

- **What's going wrong?** Lois is handing over her pupils to their parents after a day at school when the mother of nine-year-old Billy asks to speak to her; she says that Billy's gone to a friend's house for tea and asks if Lois is free to talk now. It turns into an impromptu 20-minute meeting in which the mother accuses Lois of having been rude to Billy the previous day, claiming Lois told him he was lazy. The warning lights are flashing but Lois's fight instinct kicks in. 'I said no such thing,' she says. At this point the mother asks if she's accusing Billy of lying. Realizing that it's moving into Escalation, Lois tries to back out but the mother is determined to have her say. At home that evening, Lois says to Sai that she's had enough of teaching.

- **How to fix it?** This is the worst possible scenario for Lois: an impromptu meeting, at the wrong time and in the wrong place, with a parent who's angry and upset. When this happens, the best strategy is to press the STOP! button. Lois can do this politely but firmly, by saying:

> I realize you're very upset about this, and I'm sorry if Billy was upset by any comment I made. Can we please meet tomorrow to talk it through properly? I'll ask the deputy head to join us.

It's extremely challenging to listen and respond when someone's criticism takes you by surprise, especially when you don't feel it's justified. By rescheduling their meeting, Lois has time to prepare by thinking backward from the purpose and intended outcomes, in collaboration with the deputy head. When the meeting happens, she can listen to the perspective of Billy's mother and give her own perspective without being so defensive, preventing the Big Argument and the Lock Down.

WHAT TO DO?

STEP 1:
Halve the Time and Double the Value

To remind people that meetings cost money, variations on the taxi metering system have been developed which calculate the real-time price of a meeting. Having plugged in the annual salary of your staff, you ask meeting attendees to clock in when they arrive and the meter ticks away in the corner for everyone to see. Without going to such lengths, you can still take on the challenge of halving the time you spend in meetings and doubling their value. Here are seven questions to ask:

[1] Is there a clear purpose and outcome for the meeting? If these aren't well defined, don't schedule the meeting. If you're on the invite list, ask for more information or decline the invitation.

[2] Whose meeting is it? Knowing this gives the meeting an edge. If there isn't a named person, it'll probably be a *nonversation.*

[3] Have people done the preparation that's been asked for? If not, move on to the next agenda item or stop the meeting. This way, you start to create a culture where people come prepared.

[4] Is it essential for everyone to be here? If the answer is 'no', leave the meeting yourself or make it acceptable for other people to leave. In this way, you develop a culture that discourages

Stacking. Besides, big thinking usually emerges from small groups of smart people.

[5] Do we need the allocated time? Don't plan meetings in hour-long increments just because your calendar is set up this way. Plan them to be shorter, or finish early and give people some time back.

[6] Do we need to meet in person or can we tackle the conversation remotely? Face-to-face is always preferable, but not if people are doing a half-day trip for a one-hour meeting. Schedule a conference call or video meeting instead.

[7] Have we got agreements for how we'll conduct the meeting? Set it up so that people are unequivocally in the meeting or out of it. This takes seconds and doesn't require a big lecture. My first request is for people to put their devices away. If they'd rather be on their phone, they're better off being somewhere else.

Each of these steps will help you combat the downside effects of Stacking, Spinning, Skimming and Spilling. The meeting meter will still tick, but you'll have fewer meetings and higher-quality conversations. In doing so, you can defy the words of American writer and economist Thomas Sowell, who said that people who enjoy meetings should not be in charge of anything.

Lesson 6: Time wasted in meetings can't be bought back.

Chapter 7

IDENTIFY
Motivations

HOW TO UNDERSTAND WHAT MAKES PEOPLE TICK

In the early 19th century, phrenology was all the rage. It was seen as the 'science' of being able to discern the personality of an individual by feeling and measuring the lumps and bumps on their head. The so-called fathers of phrenology, Franz Joseph Gall and Johann Spurzheim, popularized the idea that our character is linked to precise organs in the brain. One only needs to look at the title of Gall's book, published in 1819, to see the significance attached to his discovery. It was titled: *The Anatomy and Physiology of the Nervous System in General, and of the Brain in Particular, with Observations Upon the Possibility of Ascertaining the Several Intellectual and Moral Dispositions of Man and Animal, by the Configuration of Their Heads.*

The theory of phrenology was so widely believed that some employers sent prospective employees to be measured with calipers. I can only guess that a poor wretch who'd set his heart on being an accountant may have seen his hopes dashed because his brain area attributed to poetic talent protruded more than the area associated with constancy and numerical analysis.

It didn't occur to Gall and Spurzheim that they already had the most incredible method for understanding people's 'intellectual and moral dispositions', in the form of conversation. While personality profiles and other diagnostic tools have their place, there's no better way of identifying what motivates each individual person than by asking them.

WHY YOU STAY OR LEAVE

A manager at one of the world's largest companies told me that, when he first joined the organization, people were rewarded for 'getting to the top' with wall-to-wall carpet in their offices. This symbol of power was highly sought after but not always easy for the company to oversee. Let's say that a director moved to another location and you took over her office, but hadn't yet reached her pay grade, meaning that the carpet in your new office was too posh for you. Soon enough the friendly men from the facilities department would knock at your door and cut six inches *off* your carpet along each of the walls, leaving you with a super-sized rug. In the process, you'd be reminded of your place in the pecking order and theoretically incentivized to work all the harder in pursuit of success.

Almost certainly this approach demotivated more people than it motivated, and served to strengthen the resentment between the haves and the have-nots. But it also reflected a failure to understand that people are motivated in different ways. While one person is motivated by constant variety and flux, her colleague at the next desk may be motivated by stability and structure. Some employees cannot operate without high levels of acknowledgment, while others have little need for it. These are my top motivations at work, ranked in order of priority:

[1] Having a sense of freedom
[2] Taking on impossible challenges
[3] Working in partnership with people I trust and respect
[4] Feeling that I'm making a difference
[5] Expressing my creativity
[6] Being fully in communication
[7] Feeling trusted, valued and acknowledged
[8] Working on a variety of projects and tasks
[9] Learning new skills
[10] Being financially rewarded.

Of course the ranking is a subjective evaluation and your list can change along with your circumstances. However, I've found it to be remarkably constant over the years. When my motivations are being met, I love my work. When they're not, I get itchy feet or I'm plain miserable. Now I understand what to look for when I take on a commitment or project. If I can't see a big challenge, or don't feel able to make a difference, I know I'm better off going elsewhere. If there isn't room for my creative expression, I'll feel constrained and frustrated. And if I don't trust and respect the people I'm working with, I'd rather walk away. In this way my work has more chance of making an impact, and I can stay true to myself.

THE RESIGNATION LETTER

What amazes me is how many managers have never had individual conversations with their team members to understand their motivations. It's never really occurred to them to do so. Yet this is perhaps the most important conversation of all. I'm not saying that we should pander to the whims of our staff; after all, our organizations exist to serve customers and shareholders. But, if you manage people, why wouldn't you seek to understand the conditions in which they operate at their best, and then figure out how you can motivate them to deliver brilliantly on their accountabilities?

Ria relies heavily on Alex, who is a member of her operations team. Alex originally came into the industry as a software coder. Immensely motivated, he worked 60 hours a week and was soon rewarded with a growing team, an impressive salary and a handsome bonus. But the more senior he's become, the less motivated he's felt, and he's not entirely sure why. He's tried suggesting to Ria a couple of times that they reshape his role, but Ria's lost other members of her team and wants to keep Alex in his current position to provide stability. Ria is taken aback when they have this conversation one Friday morning. Alex starts by saying:

I've thought about it long and hard, and I'm handing in my resignation. I'm sorry.

 I'm shocked. I thought you were happy in your job, and you had a pay rise at the start of the year.

 I know, but it's not really about the pay.

 What is it, then?

 I'm not enjoying my work. I spend my time managing people issues, and that's not what I came into the business for.

 Is there anything we can do to persuade you to stay?

 I'm sorry, Ria. I've already accepted another job as technical director, although I'll serve out my notice period.

Ideally Ria would have stopped Spinning for long enough to understand Alex's motivations when they first started working together. Had they done so, their conversation might have begun like this:

What's important to you in your role?

It's not so much about money or success.
It's more about the technical side of the job.

When have you been at your most motivated?

It was when we started developing programs in
Java in the 1990s. We were breaking new ground
every day. When I became a manager I was told to
stay out of the detail and focus on delivering
through others. That was when I lost my spark.

So would you describe technical challenges as one
of your primary motivations?

Absolutely, no question. Without that, I'd start
looking for a different job.

If they'd kept talking, they could have drawn up the following list of
Alex's motivations:

[1] Solving difficult technical challenges
[2] Having a boss who's willing to listen to my opinion

[3] Being recognized for my contribution (not necessarily financial)

[4] Feeling I'm fairly treated, and treating others fairly

[5] Making continuous improvements

[6] Seeing how I contribute to the future of the company.

It would have been so simple for Ria and Alex to review this list on a periodic basis, but now it's too late, and in retrospect it's blindingly obvious why Alex is dispirited. He rarely gets involved in technical issues, and, despite being given a pay rise, doesn't feel thanked for his contribution. He thinks that Ria is too busy Stacking and Spinning to listen to his opinion. And to cap it all, Alex has lost sight of where the company is going and can't see how he's helping to shape its future. When these factors are combined, he feels as though he's surviving in his job rather than thriving in it. And Ria has made a cardinal mistake: she's assumed that Alex has the same motivations as herself.

SAYING THANK YOU

It's worth saying a word on internal and external recognition, which manifest in different ways. We all need acknowledgment up to a point, but people who place more emphasis on *internal* recognition are relatively unmoved when someone says they've done a good job; they're more concerned with whether they've reached their own standards. In contrast, those who are strongly motivated by *external* recognition will quickly become demoralized if they aren't hearing people's acknowledgment.

This is the case for construction manager Sai, who is worried that he's out of favour and will lose his job when Karl takes over as his boss. In fact, Karl is perfectly satisfied with the quality of Sai's work but doesn't condone thanking someone for doing what they're paid to do anyway, even if they're doing it well. In his mind, acknowledgment should be offered in exceptional circumstances, so that its value doesn't get cheapened.

Dan Ariely, a professor of psychology and behavioural economics, conducted a study in which students at the Massachusetts Institute of Technology were split into three groups and asked to perform a series of tasks that involved finding pairs of letters on a page, in return for a small financial reward. Students in the first group had to write their name on their sheet before handing it to the experimenter, who looked it over and said 'Uh huh' and put it on a pile. People in the second group didn't write their name down, and the experimenter placed their sheet on a pile without looking at it. People in the third group had their sheet shredded on completion. The students were invited to perform the next task for slightly less money, and Ariely tracked the point at which they chose to drop out of the experiment. The students whose work was shredded opted out long before the ones who were acknowledged, but the surprise was this: the people whose work was ignored reacted in almost the same way as those whose work was shredded. Ariely's conclusion was that ignoring people's efforts is akin to shredding them.[1]

WHAT TO DO?

STEP 1:
Notice What Motivates and Demotivates You

It's not difficult to figure out what your own motivations are. First, think about the jobs that you've loved the most and consider what made you feel so motivated. Now recall the ones where you've felt most demoralized. These should both point you to the same set of motivations. In the jobs you loved, your motivations were being met. In the ones you hated, they weren't.

Now notice, as you go through your working week, what's motivating and demotivating you. If you come home and say you've had a good day, why was it good? Just as important, what made your day bad? You may think it's just because 'stuff happened' or 'stuff didn't happen' but there's usually a link to motivations.

STEP 2:
Talk About Motivations

It's not enough to notice motivations: what's important is the ensuing discussion. Since your manager and colleagues aren't mind-readers, tell them how you operate at your best rather than waiting for them to ask. For example, Sai needs to talk to Karl about the importance of regular feedback. Without it, he assumes that he's doing a bad job and can get into an emotional spiral. Even if he discovers that he's not meeting Karl's expectations, he'll know what he needs to do to put things right.

If you manage people, make sure you talk about motivations in your one-to-one conversations instead of just checking on progress against goals and objectives. If Ria had done this, she could easily have reshuffled things to give Alex an additional accountability for technical assurance, talked to him about the future direction of the business and gone out of her way to thank him a little more often. The investment of time would have been tiny compared to the effort involved in interviewing, hiring and embedding Alex's replacement.

Whatever your role, you're looking for the 'sweet spot' that's a match between what the organization needs and what's motivating. There isn't always a perfect fit, but we can strive to get closer.

STEP 3:
Be Aware of the Clashes

It would be a mistake to assume that your motivations sit comfortably side-by-side; sometimes you can feel as though they're tearing you apart. I coached one executive who reached breaking point for this reason. Working in a culture of relentless pressure, she was receiving 400 emails a day and her diary was stacked before she arrived at work, guaranteeing that she would spend her day Spinning and Skimming. We identified that her top motivations in her work and personal life were 'unbridled success' and 'domesticity'. Suddenly her pain was easier to understand: unable to contemplate the possibility of failure, her solution was to work harder, extinguishing any semblance of domesticity. Anyone who struggles with their work–life balance shares this dilemma (although it must be noted that work–life balance is a flawed term, because work is part of life). As we explored my client's situation further, the analogy of the metaphorical Zen horse became very apt: perhaps she needed to slow things down rather than gallop faster.

As she drew breath and reviewed her predicament, it became self-evident that my client couldn't fulfil her motivations in her current working environment. She met with her boss and negotiated a settlement to leave the business. She found a new role that helped her career progress but was more conducive to her family circumstances. As she proved, you can start to make mindful choices about how to reconcile your motivations when you get them out in the open and discuss them. In the process, you reclaim your power.

Lesson 7: What motivates you may demotivate others.

Chapter 8

CHALLENGE
Truth

HOW TO AVOID NARROW-MINDEDNESS

Over the last couple of decades, our perceptions of what's true have been repeatedly tested. An Iraqi chemical engineer, codenamed Curveball, fed false stories about biological weapons to the American and German intelligence services prior to the Iraq War, in the hope that it would bring down Saddam Hussein's regime. His wish was fulfilled, but the premise on which the war was justified turned out to be hollow.

In 2007, analysts who predicted the end of the housing bubble were dismissed as irritating naysayers and crazy thinkers. Not long afterwards, the very people who had brushed aside the warnings struggled to prevent a total collapse of the global banking system. Nobel Prize-winning social psychologist Daniel Kahneman examined the reliability of professional forecasts by experts and concluded that they produce poorer predictions than dart-throwing monkeys, who would have made a random but evenly spread set of choices.[1]

In the late 1990s my business bible was *Built to Last* by Jim Collins and Jerry Porras. The authors studied 18 visionary companies, each of which was considered to be a crown jewel in its industry, whose collective share price had performed 15 times better than the stock market over an average period of 92 years since their incorporation. Within a decade, half of these organizations had slipped down the rankings; Collins and Porras responded by writing *How the Mighty Fall*. Another of their classic studies, *Good to Great*, has sometimes been renamed *Good to Great to Gone*, in reference to enterprises that have fallen from grace. There was nothing wrong with their research, but the world doesn't seem to be conforming to the old rules.

How do we know what or who to believe?

TALKING YOURSELF INTO A DRAMA

Funnily enough, we shouldn't always believe ourselves. Finn sits near the bottom of his respective communication chain and is hearing all sorts of rumours. He works as a civil servant and his government department works for whichever party is in power. The government is under enormous pressure to deliver on its manifesto promises and the opposition party and the media are on the hunt for vulnerabilities to exploit. This means that Finn's ultimate boss, who is a government minister, is constantly reacting to the latest political firebomb that's being thrown at her, and the reverberations of each blast can be felt all the way down to Finn's desk.

When he's in the pub on a Friday night, Finn's friends ask how his job is going, and he says:

> It's a disaster zone. We know our department's in line for the chop because it's all over the press. They keep us in the dark until the last minute and then the guillotine comes down. My boss ignores me most of the time. New vacancies in government are non-existent, so I need to start looking elsewhere.

Finn is talking in a very convincing fashion and believes he's speaking the truth of the situation. But what he says contains a pinch of facts and a large dollop of elaboration. According to the dictionary, 'truth' means 'in accordance with the facts', but if Finn could engage his rational brain, he would see that his story contains very few facts:

Facts	What Finn says
A tabloid newspaper circulated a rumour regarding £3 billion of government cuts	We know our department's in line for the chop because it's all over the press.
Finn's colleague in another department was given a month's notice of redundancy.	They keep us in the dark until the last minute and then the guillotine comes down.
His boss cancelled their last one-to-one.	My boss ignores me most of the time.
There are vacancies in some departments. Finn hasn't checked what's available.	New vacancies in government are non-existent, so I need to start looking elsewhere.

While Finn has no intention of lying, he does have good reason to exaggerate, as we all do. It allows him to canvass support for his point of view. But people's allegiance doesn't come without a cost. Each time he explains how he's the unfortunate victim of circumstances outside his control, he becomes more emotionally invested in the storyline of his own drama and feels more helpless to influence it. Finn can't see that his perspective is one of many possible versions of the truth.

Finn's thinking is influenced by his negative bias, meaning that he prepares mentally and emotionally for the worst-case scenario. This makes sense from a survival perspective, but going through life in the brace position isn't conducive to fulfilment and is pretty stressful too.

TAKING ALTERNATIVE PERSPECTIVES

We can refer to Finn's story of his situation as the first perspective, because it's his personal view. When we feel challenged or confronted, it's difficult to look beyond the first perspective because we become invested in our opinions, and we're reluctant to let go of them. But, while we think our circumstances are the problem, the biggest obstacle we need to overcome is our own thinking.

Taking the second perspective requires considering – or, better still, listening – to someone else's viewpoint. For example, if Finn sought out his boss, Lizzy, and expressed his concerns, he might be surprised at her reply:

First, I apologize for not spending enough time with you recently. I'm covering my manager's role while she's on sick leave, which means I'm doing two jobs, but I promise not to move our next meeting. As for further cuts, I've heard nothing so far to suggest our department's under threat.

Finn's been so fused to his opinions and emotions that he hasn't stopped for a second to consider things from Lizzy's perspective. Doing so dislodges his strongly held view that he's going to be made redundant and gives him a greater appreciation for the demands she is facing.

If Finn wanted to shake up his view of the situation further, he could also consider a third perspective. This would be the perspective of someone watching as an independent observer who has no personal agenda to push and no vested interest in the outcome. For example, Finn has a mentor whom he meets occasionally, and he says:

> I realize that it's difficult not to take things personally, but it sounds as though your boss is under tremendous pressure and seems to be fighting fires on every front. Perhaps her lack of attention is a reflection of her trust in you.

So which of these perspectives is true? We can conclude that there are many different versions of the truth, and no absolute truth. If I can recognize that my story is one of many, it allows me to be curious to hear yours. I might find that yours is equally valid, or even more plausible than mine. In the process, my own story becomes malleable. This is why conversation is so powerful, wherever you work, and whatever your role.

RESTORING THE RELATIONSHIP

I worked in a joint venture a few years ago where the relationship between the two organizations in the venture had become strained. Each organization had its own culture, drivers and pressures. Their staff worked in different offices, and it was convenient to blame the other organization whenever something went wrong. Small niggles escalated daily into disagreements. Over time, this created a culture of mistrust that began to jeopardize the future of the joint venture. Had it done so, the financial and reputational costs would have been catastrophic.

Recognizing that a change had to come from the top, the senior leaders from both parties agreed to get together on a monthly basis, for a complete day, to stop Spinning and to listen slowly, both of which were wholly against their nature. The objective was to appreciate each other's world rather than to seek a single version

of the truth, with no tolerance for Blamestorming, Yes, But …
or Dominatricks.

At the first meeting, each person spoke about their pressure
points, how it felt to engage with the other party, and the positive
and negative impact of each other's behaviour. As an observer, it was
like watching a dry riverbed fill with water and begin to flow again.
Something remarkable happens when you slow down for long
enough to listen to each other in this way. The natural rhythm and
balance of mindful conversation gets restored. People can pause
mid-sentence to gather their thoughts without being cut off. No time
is wasted on self-righteousness. I find conversations like this a
privilege to listen to. They restore my faith in humanity, and they
start to restore people's faith in each other.

WHAT TO DO?

STEP 1:
Listen to Each Other's Stories

When you feel stuck, imagine your issue as a sculpture on a plinth
in the middle of a room. Because a sculptor works in a three-
dimensional medium, he or she needs to give as much attention to
the back of the sculpture as the front and will consider how it looks
from above and below. In the same way, if you consider the first,
second and third perspectives when faced with a challenge, you
develop a more dynamic view of it and can avoid becoming stuck
in a single interpretation.

The best way of getting a three-dimensional perspective is to
create regular opportunities to listen to each other's stories. This is
distinct from trading opinions, coming up with solutions, devising
plans or allocating actions. All of these have their appropriate time
and place, but the first challenge is to be curious about each other's
world, which forces you to listen slowly and helps prevent myopia.

You can set up these opportunities on a semi-regular basis, either individually, as a team or between functions. Even taking an hour to stop and listen to people's stories will be repaid many times over in the deepening of relationships so long as you set the ground rules and don't let judgement and blame creep in. Start by acknowledging that you are only speaking *a* truth and not *the* truth, and then hear each other out.

STEP 2:
Agree Working Assumptions

Since none of us knows exactly what the future has in store, we rely on predictions, which in turn are based on assumptions. For example, when an entrepreneur explains how her idea is going to take the world by storm, and reels off her profit numbers for the next three years, investors may admire her confidence but they'll know the future won't pan out exactly as she's describing. The reality may be better or worse, but it will almost certainly be different. A more important question is whether her assumptions are robust and credible.

A huge proportion of Rafa's day is spent clarifying assumptions. He's managing a project to migrate customer data onto a new IT platform. It's a complicated process of developing code, testing it and eventually switching off the legacy system and going live with the new one. The project is split into multiple workstreams, some of which overlap while others must run in sequence. While Rafa's bosses are pressing him for a hard-and-fast date for going live, and a price tag to go with it, they need to understand that Rafa's answer is predicated on hundreds of assumptions. For this reason, it's vital that he and his team examine and test their assumptions. One conversation with team member Anna goes like this:

In the plan I've got 15 full-time developers
working on Phase 2 from 1 September.

Hang on a minute, we won't have that many.
Most of them will still be on Phase 1 in September.

Oh, that's not what I've got in the plan.
So what's our working assumption?

Well, let's assume we can release five developers
on 1 September, and the others can transition
at the end of the month.

To deliver any collective project successfully, you must get your assumptions out in the open. In doing so, you recognize that you're operating in a world of stories rather than truths, and you reduce the chance of stumbling into the Tangle. If circumstances change, you can update your working assumptions accordingly, but you'll be making a conscious choice to do so.

STEP 3:
Sharpen Your Storytelling Skills

Whether we're putting ourselves forward in an interview, pitching for work or chatting to friends in the pub, we're all storytellers. As you go through your week, notice the stories you're telling and the impact they're having. Rather than Skimming in a meeting, or getting stuck in Dominatricks, observe how other people's stories come to life or die a death, and how the best storytellers understand their audience, hold people's attention and manage the pace and rhythm of their interactions. More important, seek to discover your own style.

Here are five characteristics of storytelling that Rafa should keep in mind:

[1] Create a shared story: Rafa's managing a complex programme of work that relies on the collaboration of multiple internal and external parties. The chances of it delivering on time and to budget are stacked against him, with research showing that on average large IT projects run 45 per cent over budget, 7 per cent over time and deliver 56 per cent less value than expected.[2] To beat the odds, a collective story is needed, which extends way beyond the legal clauses in a partnership agreement, and which resonates across all the stakeholders, creating a shared sense of belonging.

[2] Show people the future: A great story needs to be meaningful and compelling, taking people to a different world – hence the phrase 'once upon a time …' However much you stretch the imagination of your listeners, they must believe that your story could be true. To remind people of the larger context for what they're doing, Rafa has commissioned life-sized cardboard cut-outs of customers, each of which has an identity and a corresponding narrative. He has a moment of pride whenever he hears developers referring to customers by name when discussing technical requirements.

[3] Understand your audience: Your story needs to penetrate into the life of your listeners so they say: 'Yes, me too!' This isn't easy because Rafa's audience ranges from his company bosses, to the sales teams, to their software developers in China. He must adapt his story to address their considerations while maintaining a core message, like a golden thread, that binds them all together. Since Rafa can't be everywhere at once, his listeners will need to pass the story on, making it their own in the process. It must evolve and be retold many times without losing its essence.

[4] **Describe the challenge**: The tradition of storytelling usually involves a protagonist who faces a challenge to overcome the odds and defeat an antagonist. In Rafa's case the antagonists are market bullies – in the form of competitors – who are hoping to pillage his heartland and steal his customers. In this way, tension is created between opposing forces. The challenge can never be trivial; it requires pluck and courage, and an inner struggle needs to be overcome in order to fulfil the outer struggle. By continually making connections between the future and the current reality, the challenge is crystallized.

[5] **Strive for simplicity**: The best stories will leave you with a simple and memorable message. Don't overcook them.

It's easy to forget in our technological age that human existence was built on storytelling. It mostly happens now in meeting rooms and coffee shops, rather than round the fire, but we need it more than ever because we're struggling to keep sight of the context for what we're doing. Without meaning, our passion for our work will wither and die.

Lesson 8: Share stories rather than arguing over the truth.

Chapter 9

CLAIM
Your
POWER

WHY YOU CAN HAVE POWER WHEN YOU DON'T HAVE AUTHORITY

Early in my career, I was given the challenge to cold-call company directors and sell large-scale consulting programmes to them. Either I was hopeless, or the task was absurdly ambitious – or both – but I got used to being cut off mid-sentence. One day, in a moment of bravado, and taking a deep breath, I called the CEO's office of a billion-pound FTSE 100 business. His assistant asked who I was and I hesitantly replied, 'It's ... er ... Rob Kendall.' Thinking I'd said 'Sir Rob Kendall', there was a momentary pause and then the CEO came on the line and greeted me like an old golfing buddy.

The subsequent conversation unravelled at great speed. Having unexpectedly reached the pinnacle of my cold-calling career on the back of a Mixed Message, I reached its low point a few seconds later when the CEO realized his mistake. Furious at having been embarrassed, he gave me a double-barrelled lecture on time-wasting. It was probably a good thing, because I was soon moved on to other duties. Even so, I briefly experienced the influence that comes from having a title in front of your name.

THE INFLUENCE OF AUTHORITY

The impact of authority on people's behaviour was famously highlighted in the 1960s by social psychologist Stanley Milgram, who conducted a series of startling experiments at Yale University. Volunteers were told that they would be contributing to a study on the effects of punishment on learning, and would be either a 'teacher' or a 'pupil' in a game of word pairs. The twist was that the teacher would administer an electric shock each time the pupil gave a wrong answer.

Having rigged the process so that the research volunteer was always the teacher who gave the shocks, the pupil – a trained actor – was strapped to a chair in the adjacent room, with electrodes seemingly attached, and the experiment began. As incorrect responses mounted, the teacher was told to increase the electric shocks in increments from 15 volts up to a peak of 450 volts. The highest switch was ominously marked 'XXX'.

If the volunteer indicated their desire to halt the experiment, the experimenter gave them a series of verbal prompts that escalated from polite insistence to outright exertion of authority:

[1] Please continue.
[2] The experiment requires that you continue.
[3] It is absolutely essential that you continue.
[4] You have no other choice, you must go on.

Milgram confidently predicted that the volunteers would refuse to continue as soon as it became apparent that they were causing distress to the pupil. But he hugely underestimated the power of the spoken word by an authority figure. In one of the studies 65 per cent of the volunteers abandoned their values in the face of Dominatricks, going the whole way to the 'XXX' switch while the pupil screamed wildly in the adjacent room.

Later experiments revealed how the influence of authority manifested in the workplace. In one of them, a 'doctor' called 22 hospitals and instructed the duty nurse to administer a drug that hadn't been prescribed for that ward, in a dosage that was twice the maximum recommended on the container. Although the nurses knew that prescriptions were never to be given over the phone, 21 out of 22 began to prepare the drug because they'd been instructed to do so by a doctor.[1] Deference to authority seemed to have a greater influence on their behaviour than consideration of the moral consequences of their actions.

Moving forward to 10 April 2010, the Polish president and 95 other top political, military, financial and religious leaders were killed in a plane crash while travelling to a Second World War memorial service near Smolensk in Russia. Visibility was appalling and an air traffic controller had told the flight crew 25 minutes before the crash: 'The conditions for landing do not exist.' So why did they go ahead? The investigation by the Interstate Aviation Committee concluded that the pilots had been subjected to pressure by high-ranking passengers to land the plane rather than divert to another airport and delay the memorial service. At one point in the black-box recording, the director of diplomatic protocol for the Ministry of Foreign Affairs was heard entering the cockpit and was told by the pilot, 'Sir, the fog is increasing. At the moment, under these conditions that we have now, we will not manage to land.' The reply was, 'Well, then we have a problem.'[2]

THE SAFETY MEETING

We mustn't forget that the volunteers in the Milgram experiment, the nurses who took instruction from a so-called doctor, and the captain who was flying the presidential plane all had the power to say 'no'. Please don't misunderstand me: I'm not saying it would have been easy to do so. But Milgram's volunteers could have exercised their right to walk out. The nurses could have categorically stated that they weren't willing to go against their training and put the life of a patient on the line. And the captain could have insisted on following the recommendation of air traffic control not to attempt to land the plane, protecting 96 lives. In each case, under the influence of an authority figure, a conversation went horribly wrong and people strayed from their values.

Construction manager Sai has his own challenge in this regard. He has been passionately communicating the message that 'Safety is our number one priority' on his construction sites for years. A man died on a previous project where Sai was construction manager, and even though he wasn't personally at fault, Sai still feels responsible because it happened on his watch. On this project, he's worked tirelessly to encourage his men to stand up to anyone who isn't putting safety first, irrespective of their rank, but it involves having difficult conversations on a daily basis.

On this particular morning, Sai is feeling stressed. Six trucks have arrived to pour concrete and there's a problem with them accessing the site. Things get worse when he bumps into Karl, his boss:

Sai, don't forget we've got a client meeting in 20 minutes.

OK, but we've got an issue with the concrete pour, so I may be late.

Sai, I need you at the meeting. The client may have questions about the schedule.

Where are we having it?

In the induction room. It's the only one big enough.

But there's a safety meeting happening in there.

Then move it out!

Sai's very uncomfortable about moving the safety meeting but he succumbs to Karl's authority. He sticks his head round the door of the induction room and says:

Guys, I'm really sorry, we need to move you out of here in a few minutes. We've got an urgent client meeting. There should be space in the corner of the office if you want to gather round a desk there.

As construction offices are temporary structures and notoriously short on meeting space, the people who were turfed out of the induction room struggled to find another spot to park themselves. By lunchtime, people across the site were saying: 'Safety is our number one priority? Really? What a joke!' In their eyes, Sai's credibility was shot, even though he was only following Karl's instructions.

The irony of this situation is that Karl's also very committed to people being safe on his project but, because he's Spinning, he doesn't step back to think about the consequences of his behaviour. By virtue of his role, people on his site will pay close attention to what he does, says and asks. In equal measure, they'll draw conclusions from what he *doesn't* do, say or ask. This comes with the territory when you're in a position of authority. Under pressure, he's not thinking about the consequences of his actions and needs Sai to remind him what he's really committed to.

So what could Sai have done differently? Although Karl has more authority than him, Sai *does* have the power to decline Karl's request, or make a counter-offer, or both, in which case the conversation could go like this:

But there's a safety meeting happening in there.

 Then move it out!

Karl, I can hand over the site issues and be at the meeting, but I'm not going to turf people out of the induction room. We keep asking our people to prioritize safety over commercial issues, and this is a chance to demonstrate that we mean it.

 OK, so what's the solution?

I'll call the client and explain the situation. We may need to start with a site tour, and then move into the meeting room.

There are several reasons why this works so much better. First, Sai doesn't obfuscate his 'no' behind a load of explanation or make any apologies for it. In doing so, he is making a clear stand. Second, Sai explains the context for declining and reminds Karl of the value they place on safety, which they have both committed to; in this respect, he's actually doing Karl a favour. And third, Sai looks for a solution to the problem that allows them to have the best of both worlds by sticking to their values and still meeting with the client. He has found his voice without surrendering his power.

AUTHORITY AND POWER

A cartoon shows an employee standing to attention in front of his boss's desk. Leaning back in his executive swivel chair, the boss says, 'Come in Frank. I've been meaning to communicate downward to you.'

This brings us to the difference between authority and power, terms that are often (wrongly) used interchangeably. Authority flows downward, from top to bottom. In his site world, Karl has the most authority, and then Sai has slightly less authority, and Sai's supervisors have less again, and so the process goes on. But power is an altogether different phenomenon and can't be neatly mapped out on an organization chart. It's the ability to direct or influence the behaviour of others or the course of events, and therefore it has the potential to flow in any direction – up, down or sideways – depending on where the power resides.

Of course, some kinds of power go hand-in-hand with authority. If you hold a higher rank than someone, you hold the purse strings and have the power to threaten or reward them. But rank and power can't buy you the respect and motivation of your employees. This is why so many efforts to change fail; if the case for change is unconvincing, or if trust is absent, people won't invest energy and commitment in it. Once you've lost their listening, your power becomes hollow. Autocrats fear, above all, the power of a group whose collective voice threatens their position and their identity. Because they have limited goodwill to draw on, they exercise their rank all the harder.

Looked at this way, Sai in many respects has more power than Karl, because he has stronger relationships with the men on site and more years of experience, too. He works alongside the supervisors every day and knows every tradesman by name. If he accedes to Karl's instruction, Sai will surrender his power. Instead, he can influence Karl's thinking by reminding him of his values. If Karl is worth his salt as a leader, he'll be grateful to Sai for doing so.

WHAT TO DO?

STEP 1:
Exercise Your Power to Say 'No'

A request and a demand are not the same, but we often get them confused in our mind. A demand leaves you with no room to decline and is the same as saying, 'Do what I say, or else.' A request is just that; it must leave you the freedom to accept, decline or make a counter-offer. While we all worry about the consequences of challenging an authority figure, we often have more wriggle room than we think to decline or negotiate an acceptable solution.

If you're in the habit of Stacking too many commitments and feel overwhelmed as a consequence, try saying 'no' to twice as many requests or negotiating the terms of your agreements. This doesn't mean you become bolshy and obstructive, but does mean that you think more carefully before saying 'yes', especially if your integrity will be compromised, your stress levels will skyrocket and your productivity will be affected. The most common way people surrender their power is by thinking they can't negotiate.

STEP 2:
Create a Culture of Challenge

If you manage a team, function or organization, make it as easy as possible for people to voice their concerns and questions without fear of being penalized for doing so. For this to happen, you'll need to start by having conversations about what people can and can't challenge. When they start testing if you are true to your word, it's crucial to demonstrate that you're willing to listen rather than going on the defensive. By publicly acknowledging and rewarding people for speaking up, you start to shift the culture of your organization.

I worked with the project leaders and construction managers who were building the stadiums for the 2012 Olympic Games. They were passionately committed to delivering the first ever Olympics in which nobody was killed during the construction process – a tough challenge given that the project required 46,000 people to do 77 million hours of work. Meeting me at the security entrance one morning, the head of health and safety said: 'I've just had a difficult conversation with my boss. He was livid with me for not challenging him hard enough on safety.' This comment summed up the culture on site. They weren't inviting each other to question and challenge their thinking; they were demanding it.

If people go along with flawed ideas, rather than challenging them, the consequences can be very costly. In the run-up to the May 2015 general election in the UK, Ed Miliband, the leader of the Labour Party, unveiled a giant 2-ton stone on which six election promises for the Labour Party had been chiselled. The idea was to emphasize that Labour would stick to its pledges in granite-like fashion if it was voted in. When the story went public, some viewers thought it was a hoax and one report claimed that a Labour Party official screamed at the television. Within minutes social media went mad with comparisons between Ed Miliband and Moses. Thanks to Photoshop, the list of pledges was changed into a giant shopping list, so that 'A country where the next generation do better than the last' became 'Check with Justine if we need loo rolls'. After the election, the 'Edstone' was apparently spirited away to a warehouse in South London, and time will tell whether it's ground into pebbles for someone's driveway or becomes a museum piece.

The question this story raises is how on earth the stone was approved in the first place. An aide claimed that it got through 10 planning meetings without anyone challenging it, presumably because Ed Miliband, who was in the highest position of authority, was in favour of it.[3] It's easy for us to pour scorn in hindsight, but it raises the question of whether you are able to challenge each other's truth.

The starting point is to develop ground rules on how you'll conduct your conversations with each other. If you have an agreement to constructively challenge each other, it's more likely that someone will speak up when they disagree with your position. The notion that leaders and managers are all-seeing and all-knowing is outdated and frankly ludicrous. Their job is to unlock the knowledge in their organization, which resides in the heads of their employees. We're all going to make better decisions if we can test and challenge each other's thinking.

Lesson 9: Never underestimate your power.

Chapter 10

ADAPT Your STYLE

HOW TO UNDERSTAND SOMEONE'S PREFERRED STYLE OF COMMUNICATION

In 350 BC, Aristotle wrote his *Nicomachean Ethics*, in which he gave his views on justice and fairness. He argued that it's impossible to apply the rigid rules of the law to every situation in life; sometimes we need to be more flexible in our approach. To illustrate his point, he referred to a 'rule', made of pliable lead, used by stonemasons on the island of Lesbos. Since it could be easily bent, but would hold its shape, this simple and ingenious device could be used to measure or copy the shape of an irregular piece of stone or a column. Well over 2,000 years later, Aristotle's metaphor of 'bending the rules' is firmly woven into our language.[1] Although we tend to use it in the sense of defying convention, his main point was about flexible thinking.

When we're interacting, we face the challenge of how to remain true to ourselves while adapting the way we speak and listen to suit that person or situation. This can be a tricky balance to strike, but it's made easier if we can appreciate that people have different preferred styles of communication. You may favour a structured approach to conversation, while your client uses it as a means of creative expression. Your natural thinking style may be strategic while your colleague's is tactical. You may be thoughtful and reflective while your boss is decisive. In this way, you have the potential to complement each other well, but equally your different styles may clash, leading you to make judgements about each other's character.

A CLASH OF PREFERENCES

At the age of 45, Lois has taught for 20 years and she feels battle-weary. She's highly respected by her colleagues, but the pleasure of teaching has been dulled by having to focus on tests and targets.

Having talked – mainly moaned – to her partner Sai about this for several months, she's resolved to chat to Matt, her headteacher. He's been in place for nine months and is taking a very business-like approach to things. He seems to spin from one meeting to the next, but she's finally got 20 minutes in his diary.

Their conversation starts like this:

Thanks for taking the time to see me. I've been giving my role a lot of thought over the last few months and ... um ... I feel it may be time for a change. I'm not saying I want to leave the school or anything. After all, I've been here for 10 years and ...

I see. I'm sure we can sort something out.

Well, yes, that would be great if we can find a way ...

It's good timing because I'd like you to organize some science trips. I've got a small fund for new projects, and I've also got a governors' meeting next month where I can put forward a proposal. I don't see any reason to delay things.

OK, well, that's certainly something to think about.

> It goes without saying that we want to keep you here. The constraints on pay mean that we can't offer you any more money, but I hope we can come up with ways to give you fresh challenges.

After a few more minutes, Matt proposes an action to review progress in a fortnight's time. He asks Lois to write down her recommendations and email them to him.

TIPPING INTO JUDGEMENTS

Afterwards, Matt thinks it's been a productive meeting but Lois feels flattened and thinks they've had a nonversation. In her view, he showed no interest in what was bothering her, failed to listen and engaged in Dominatricks. She disliked the way he used the term 'we' when he said, '*we* want to keep you', and '*we* can't offer you more money'. 'He sounded like my bank manager or a corporate consultant,' she thinks.

On Matt's side, he's glad that Lois has come to him and that they've agreed a plan of action, but he's got a slight concern that she seemed unclear and hesitant. 'As a member of my leadership team, she's not very proactive,' he says to himself.

To figure out why their conversation's gone wrong, we need to understand their preferences. Lois's style of communication is all about affinity. Being an excellent listener herself, and highly sensitive to visual and non-verbal cues, she dislikes it when people cut across her or don't listen. If a solution is put forward, she wants to think about it and discuss it with people she trusts before coming to a conclusion. While this might take a little longer, her decisions are well considered and she stands by them.

The emphasis for Matt is on forward momentum. When Lois is speaking, he's thinking about actions and solutions. Conversations work better for him if he understands the intended outcome at the outset. He also prefers people to come to him with options or recommendations rather than problems; if they don't, he's likely to come up with solutions on their behalf. While Lois talks about how she *feels*, Matt talks about how he *thinks*. Neither communication style is right or wrong but they are different, and that increases the likelihood of Mixed Messages.

Matt doesn't have bad intentions. He just communicates in his preferred style, but this doesn't work for Lois. On the back of their meeting, they both draw conclusions about each other's personality. As these turn into judgements, communication between them becomes increasingly strained. Matt tells his deputy that Lois was 'a bit all over the place' when he met with her. Lois refers to Matt as 'the head robot' when she's at home. Although they agree some further actions at their subsequent meeting, Lois still feels that Matt has fundamentally missed the point by failing to understand how she feels: demoralized, frustrated and unsupported. What's more, she has little confidence things will be better if she raises the issue again.

BEING FLEXIBLE

Lois and Matt need to recognize that their preferred way of communicating isn't necessarily the 'right' way. They also need to follow the principle of Aristotle's rule and be flexible enough to adjust their style. A lawyer can't expect a positive response if he says to his 12-year-old daughter, 'I put it to you that you haven't done the washing-up for two weeks', even though he talks like this all day in court. We have to adapt and, when we do, we get a better response from people.

If Matt understands Lois's preferences, he'll know that when she comes to him with a problem, the priority is for her to feel heard.

He'll also know that she needs time and space to mull over a conversation before getting to a decision. Equally, Lois will know that it works to be direct with Matt and to tell him what she needs from him. Taking this into account, Lois would open their conversation like this:

> Thanks for taking the time to see me. I'm not happy in my role at the moment. To be clear, I don't want to leave the school and I do want to find a solution, but first of all I need you to listen. Can we chat about this now, or is it better to talk at more length another time?

Lois has given Matt a much clearer steer with this opening. Because she's adapted her style of communication, she gets a better response from him. If Matt is aware of Lois's preferences, and his own, he could say:

> First of all, Lois, thanks for letting me know. Let's take 20 minutes now for me to understand how you're feeling, and then we'll plan a longer meeting. I'll try to listen without rushing headlong into action.

This simple change prevents them from getting into Mixed Messages and ending up in the Bad Place.

REVERTING TO TYPE

When you're under pressure, which is probably much of the time, you're likely to revert to your default style of communication. If you tend to seek control, you may become directive precisely when you need to listen. If you like to understand the detail, you may become obsessed with sticking to your plan, even though the situation calls for you to be flexible.

I once worked with a leadership team whose challenge was to transform their branch network. In many ways they were perfectly suited to the task they'd been set, but I was concerned that their collective preferences were lopsided, like a seesaw with all the weight at one end. In light of this, I reminded them that they were highly task oriented and would look for pace. I warned them that they might forget to step back, look out for each other and listen to the concerns and questions of their people. And I emphasized that the similarity in their preferences could lead to issues around control, accountability and power.

Taking this challenge on the chin, they came up with three strategies in addition to their regular operational structures. The first was to have a biannual strategy meeting as a team to take stock and look further ahead. The second was to conduct quarterly communication sessions with all their staff. And the third was to have a regular social catch-up.

For the next nine months they were Stacking, Spinning and Skimming to get their business back into shape. While they made great strides forward, they cancelled their strategy meeting, didn't organize the communication sessions with their staff and didn't at any point meet up socially. In other words, they reverted to their preferences. As a consequence, their employee engagement scores were the lowest on record, some of their staff instigated grievance procedures and there were open disputes in meetings between their respective teams. The lesson from this is that you have to make a conscious effort to adapt your style when you're under pressure or when you're busy. And being busy doesn't seem likely to go away anytime soon.

WHAT TO DO?

STEP 1:
Listen to Language

Start seeing people's language as a clue to how they want you to communicate with them. For example, when Matt says, 'let's crack on', or 'cutting to the point', or 'let's find a way forward', as he frequently does, he is indicating that speed and momentum are important to him. And when Lois says, 'that's certainly something to think about', she is flagging that she'll need time to consider what Matt's saying.

A simple technique is to stop Skimming and listen to how people phrase their questions. Those of us who are highly action oriented will tend to ask *what* needs to happen. People who love plans, process and structure will ask *how* it will happen. Those who want to understand the context and purpose for doing something will ask *why* it needs to happen. And people who are very collegiate will ask *who* needs to be involved for it to happen. Of course you use all of these questions at different times, but you'll use some more regularly than others. When you understand what's important for someone, you can adapt your communication style accordingly.

STEP 2:
Pay Attention to Pace

Some people seem to conduct their conversations with their foot on the accelerator. Taking a no-frills approach, they value brevity, never giving you a paragraph if a sentence will do, and they'll metaphorically drum their fingers on the table if you don't get directly to the point. When speaking to them, it's wise to start by telling them the outcome you want and then offer recommendations and options. Otherwise, they'll become impatient, and you'll lose their attention.

Others rattle through their conversations in a more loquacious and free-spirited fashion. They zigzag their way through interactions while they think aloud. You may desperately want to keep bringing them back to the point, but it's important not to close them down too quickly or belittle their contribution.

You'll also have colleagues who take a methodical and deliberate approach to conversation. They'll speak more slowly because they view it as a reflective process. When dealing with them, it's important to make time for their questions and concerns. If you don't give them space to think, you may get their compliance but you won't get their full support. These people will often consolidate their thinking after a conversation, instead of during it, and therefore it's worth making the effort to ask for their subsequent reflections. What they say will be worth listening to.

STEP 3:
Determine Depth

The next time you go into a meeting, notice how some people gravitate toward the detail. They'll want to understand the process, the plan and the underpinning data before embarking on a course of action. If you're presenting information to them, don't expect them to follow a whim. You'll need to know your facts and have your supporting evidence if you want their commitment.

Others will glaze over when you start discussing plans and numbers. As long as the broad direction feels instinctively right, they're happy to work out the detail as they go along. When talking to them, it helps to keep things at a high level, or they will zone out.

Neither approach is intrinsically correct, and both are appropriate in different situations. It's important to remember that the person whose communication style is most different to yours may be the one who's most important to your success. If you can value their contribution and adapt your communication style when talking to them, your relationships will be stronger and your productivity will be higher. If you start by listening slowly, and paying attention to language, pace and depth, you'll develop greater flexibility. Just like Aristotle's rule.

Lesson 10: Don't assume that people want to communicate in your style.

Chapter 11

ASK Brilliant QUESTIONS

WHY YOUR QUESTIONS ARE MORE IMPORTANT THAN YOUR SOLUTIONS

At the age of 87, one of the world's most revered sports coaches was finally persuaded to share the contents of a small well-worn notebook that contained a lifetime of scribbled tips and anecdotes. When it appeared in print, *Harvey Penick's Little Red Book* became the world's bestselling sports book. How so? For starters, it was more human, inspiring and engaging than a dreary technical manual. Then there was the fact that Penick's passion for golf was evident on every page. But above all, he understood people, and even allowed himself to love them.

Whether he was coaching a world champion or a weekend hacker, Penick recognized that throwing information at them willy-nilly would ruin their game. When it came to advice, his guiding principle was that 'less is more'. My favourite story involved a lawyer of average ability who came to the great teacher for a lesson before competing in a golf match in Florida. The lawyer had a habit of over-analysing his game, and Penick suspected that technical advice would only make things worse. Needing time to think, Penick changed his approach midway through the lesson. He asked the lawyer to hit a pile of balls and retreated behind a bush to observe his pupil's golf swing from a distance, after which he went home. The lawyer was understandably bewildered and indignant at this disappearing trick. What he didn't realize was that Penick spent the afternoon sitting in his chair at home, thinking about the man's swing. After several hours, Penick concluded that the best thing for his pupil's game would be reassurance and, since he was hard of hearing, asked his wife to ring the lawyer. 'Harvey has been sitting here for hours, thinking about you,' Helen Penick said. 'And he said for me to tell you this – go to Florida and have a good time, you'll do just fine.'[1]

Two weeks later, the man came back and thanked Penick; he had won his match. With characteristic humility, Penick noted that he should be thanking the lawyer for reminding him that the student's listening is more important that the teacher's speaking. There's so much to learn from this story. Faced with a challenge, do you sit with a question, as Harvey Penick did, or go straight for an answer and jump in with your advice? For most of us, it takes more self-control to step back than to react. The more you know, the harder it is to bite your lip.

QUESTIONS, NOT ANSWERS

Innovations and discoveries come from people who are willing to sit with a question. In 1666 Isaac Newton asked, 'If the apple falls, does the moon also fall?' In 1905 Albert Einstein asked, 'What would happen if I rode a beam of light?' In 1984 a university genetics researcher called Alec Jeffreys discovered the potential of DNA fingerprinting while asking, 'How can we trace genes through family lineages?' These examples are all well and good, but they don't sit comfortably with our world of Spinning and Skimming. When we're already overwhelmed, we gravitate toward closing things off rather than opening them up. We want the feeling of certainty and control that comes from having solutions and actions. Besides, asking questions feels like an indulgence that we don't have time for.

Zoe has built up her business from an idea over a few glasses of wine to an acclaimed communications and live-events agency. Clients pay for the benefit of her wisdom and experience, and she knows her business and her market inside out. Like most business founders, Zoe has a corner-shop mentality that's both a blessing and a curse, and it works like this. When she started the company, she pitched for every piece of work, attended every client meeting and did a crash course in business management in her evenings and weekends. Her hard work was rewarded with loyal customers, a modest profit and the resources to employ more full-time staff. For each new employee, Zoe knew more about their job than they did, and this made it difficult for her to let go. Rather than stopping to explain everything, or taking the time to ask questions, she found it easier to jump in and do it herself.

Now Zoe's company has grown to a size where she can't possibly control it all personally, and her corner-shop mentality no longer works. Each project has a client director and a campaign manager, and their job is to manage their accounts. She's out of touch with the latest technologies and employs specialists whose expertise far exceeds hers. Even so, her default response is to take personal ownership of problems rather than empowering her staff to resolve them. In this sense, her actions are well intended but ultimately misplaced.

STEPPING IN

During Zoe's weekly team meeting, client manager Ed raises an issue:

We could have a big problem with the Zodiac campaign. Their new marketing director wants to put everything on hold while she reviews their requirements. We don't know whether she's got another agency that she wants to bring in.

That doesn't sound good. Well, you'll need to get in front of her as soon as possible. I'll come along too. Let's meet this week to prepare.

With the best of intentions, Zoe has managed to close the conversation down and will oversee Ed's preparation for the Zodiac meeting. When they get together, she does most of the speaking and he does most of the listening, out of respect for her experience and authority. A subtle but significant shift has taken place. Zoe has stepped in to take control of the problem and Ed is now her understudy even though he is technically still accountable for the client contract. He feels usurped and demoralized, because one of his top motivations is feeling trusted to deliver on his role. Zoe is completely oblivious to this. In fact, the old adrenalin has kicked in and she loves the feeling that she's stepping in to solve an issue – it's much more interesting than doing high-level strategy work and reviewing the company forecasts. If she could only stop Spinning and think about how to empower Ed, she might change her approach.

CHANGING THE EMPHASIS

While Zoe has a wealth of expertise to offer, she'd benefit from following the example of Harvey Penick, who would focus more on the questions he could ask than the solutions he could offer, thereby placing the emphasis on the pupil rather than the teacher. Zoe could start off like this.

Let me check first of all. You're saying that Zodiac are putting future work on hold while the new marketing director reviews her requirements, and we don't know what the outcome will be. Is that right?

 Yes, exactly.

So, what are the questions that you need to resolve?

 Umm ... let's see. There's probably a whole load of things I'm not clear on. To start with, I don't know if our current campaign, which runs to the end of the month, will be affected or not.

OK. What are your other questions?

Zoe does well not to offer solutions to each question, even though she has plenty of opinions about what Ed should do. Instead, her aim is to support his thought process. Although to some extent she's leading the conversation, there's no attempt on her part to take control of the issue. After Ed has identified several more questions, Zoe moves on as follows:

What's needed for you to answer each of your questions?

 Well, the first question was whether our current campaign will be affected. I can find out the answer to that by speaking to Max, who's the Zodiac campaign manager ...

Zoe's questions help Ed get clear in his own mind. Far from consuming hours of time, Zoe's conversation only takes a few minutes. Perhaps this is her main job as CEO: to help her managers find their own power and their own voice. She's following the example of Peter Drucker, often referred to as the founder of modern management, who trusted that his questions would be more powerful than his answers. At the age of 83, Drucker was asked by Coca-Cola to produce a report on their marketing, business and management challenges. With 29 books to his name, and a glittering reputation, he could have stuffed his report with advice, but he started his introduction like this:

> *This report raises questions. It does not attempt to give answers. It is written by an outsider who does not presume to know what the Coca-Cola Company does, what it has already decided to do or not do, let alone what it should do.*[2]

Toward the end of their conversation, Zoe asks if Ed needs any further support, and he proposes another meeting later in the week. Now it's at his request rather than hers, and there's no confusion about where the accountability lies. When he meets the new Zodiac marketing director, he asks Zoe to come along too and, although she contributes, she recognizes that it's Ed's conversation and observes his newfound poise.

WHAT TO DO?

STEP 1:
Shift Your Ratio of Advice to Questions

Oscar Wilde claimed that the only good thing to do with advice is pass it on, because it's never any use to oneself. When we pass it on, it's probably of little use to the recipient. We ought to know better, having ignored most of the advice imposed on us by parents and teachers as we grew up. In all probability, the teachers who had the greatest influence on your education were the ones who encouraged you to think for yourself and who engaged your curiosity. In those subjects, you took ownership of your learning.

If you're a specialist consultant, a financial adviser or a product specialist in a retail store, then you're paid for your advice and there's every chance it will be valued. But unsolicited advice is a different matter, and a good rule of thumb is that if it isn't asked for, it isn't wanted. There's a mini-chapter in Harvey Penick's book titled, 'When to Offer Golf Advice to Your Spouse'. The content of the chapter is three words long and reads, 'If he asks.' Such wisdom is probably the reason why so many readers claim his books have improved their life as well as their golf.

Take on shifting your ratio of advice to questions. Let's say that you have a ratio of 2:1 in favour of giving advice rather than asking questions. Accept the challenge of turning this into an equal ratio, and then see if you can move it to a 1:2 ratio. This will force you to think of your role in a completely different way. I invariably find that people come up with much better solutions for their issues or projects than I could possibly have thought of.

STEP 2:
Ask 'What's Needed?'

Whenever we have an unfulfilled expectation, our instinctive reaction is to conclude that there's something wrong and engage in Blamestorming. There's no mileage in going down this path. To counteract it, try asking 'What's needed?' It's such a simple and powerful question, because it contains no judgement and makes people focus on the outcome they want, and how to get there.

A man once told me how he went into a florist's with a £10 note and asked for a bunch of flowers. The conversation went like this:

Can you give me some flowers for £10?

I'm sorry, our bouquets start at £20.

I only have £10. Could you take some flowers out?

No, I'm sorry.

What about the roses? Can I buy those individually?

No, I'm afraid they're in bunches and start at £15.

OK. So what's needed for me to spend £10 in this shop?

Well, I could give you a few tulips with some pittosporum foliage and lily grass.

When you ask what's needed, it shifts the direction of the conversation. The other person can't give a 'yes' or 'no' response, and it's also hard for them to give their opinion. Start by making this a habit in your own conversations. By asking yourself – and others – what's needed, you begin to rewire the default tendency to look for someone or something to blame.

STEP 3:
Seek Feedback

Find out how you're doing. It's better to know, even if it's difficult to hear. It's so simple and straightforward to ask people what they want you to do more of, less of, or to continue doing. This doesn't require waiting for an appraisal or a formal assessment to come along. Turn it into a regular conversation with your boss, your team and your colleagues. Better still, have it with your customers.

Receiving feedback reminds you that there's always more to learn. Tom Kite, who was a student of Harvey Penick and topped the world golf rankings in the 1980s, remarked how his teacher learned something new about golf every day. Penick's secret was to ask brilliant questions. It kept him humble and it made him wise.

Lesson 11: Your questions are worth more than your advice.

Chapter 12

VALUE
Gender
DIFFERENCES

WHY CONVERSATIONS BETWEEN MEN AND WOMEN GO WRONG

Here is a famous brainteaser:

> A father and his son are in a car accident. The father is killed and the son is seriously injured. The son is in a critical condition and is rushed to the hospital. He's just about to go under the knife when the surgeon sees him and says, 'I cannot operate, because this boy is my son.' How can this be?

This question has been around for decades, but most people still struggle to figure it out. When producers of *Good Morning America* tested members of the public, they found that the younger the person being asked, the more likely they were to realize that the surgeon could be the boy's mother. The riddle demonstrates how our assumptions define our thinking.

Deborah Tannen, professor of linguistics at Georgetown University, and one of the world's leading experts on language and gender, recounted a similar story. She was working in her office late one evening when a woman came in and asked if she could use Tannen's phone. A few minutes later, the woman was back in search of stationery, before crashing in a third time to ask if she could leave a paper with Tannen for one of the other professors. Eventually, everything became clear: 16 out of 18 professors were male and the woman assumed that Tannen was the secretary, even though her name was clearly marked on the door.[1]

The challenge for many women is how to find their voice, and what form their voice should take, in an environment that's skewed toward male ways of communicating. A number of years ago I worked with an international oil and gas company that had one

woman among its entire senior management community. After
a strategy meeting, the conversation at dinner deteriorated to the
point where I felt uncomfortable on her behalf. She happened to
be sitting next to me, so I asked her how she coped. 'I behave like
a man,' she whispered. In all probability, none of the men felt there
was any problem; if challenged, they would have said, 'It's fine,
she's one of us.'

AFFINITY VERSUS INDEPENDENCE

Our age, family circumstances, ethnicity and location all combine
to influence the way we communicate. In addition, factors such
as introversion and extroversion have a bearing (there are slightly
more male than female introverts). It's therefore unhelpful and
untrue to make universal statements about conversational
differences between men and women. As Deborah Tannen points
out, differences are a matter of degree rather than absolute
difference. Even so we cannot ignore that some characteristics are
true for a *greater proportion* of men than women in a Western
culture, and vice versa.

Women tend to have a greater focus on maintaining affinity,
connectivity and group consensus than men. Tannen refers to this
as 'rapport-talk'. This manifests in different ways:

- Women have a greater propensity to ask questions.[2] In research
based on 100,000 interviews by John Gray and Barbara Annis,
80 per cent of women said they prefer to ask questions even when
they know the answer, because this encourages others to give
input and helps to build consensus.[3]
- Women tend to facilitate the flow of conversation more than men.
For example, both men and women use interruptions, overlaps
and minimal responses such as 'mmm', 'yeah' and 'oh', but they
do so for different purposes. Women tend to use them as a way of

showing support and encouragement to the speaker, while men more frequently use them for the opposite reason, as a way of demonstrating expertise, driving the conversation forward, competing for status or even discouraging interaction.[4]

- Women use more pronouns than men, such as 'I', 'you' and 'we'. Having analysed 400,000 texts – including blogs, essays, chat-room discussions and instant messages, Professor James W Pennebaker estimated that, on average, women use 85,000 more pronouns a year than men. This is significant because pronouns are used in reference to relationships and people.[5]
- Rather than giving orders, women are more likely to make suggestions or proposals, in line with the principles of rapport and affiliation.

Men have a higher tendency toward what Tannen calls 'report-talk'. Thirty years of study on her part have proved that women are more likely to walk away from a conversation thinking about its impact on their sense of connection with the other person, while men are more inclined to wonder whether a conversation has put them in a 'one-up' or a 'one-down' position.[6] In this way, men's talk has more consideration for hierarchy, with the following characteristics:

- They have a stronger focus on maintaining independence and avoiding vulnerability than women. For this reason, men can have a tendency to rely on their own resources instead of asking for help, and are more likely to seek individual credit rather than deflecting acknowledgment onto a wider group.
- Men are more prone to interrupting a speaker or challenging a comment than women, and more likely to ignore a comment or to respond unenthusiastically.
- While women tend to use more pronouns, men use more articles such as 'a' and 'the', in reference to objects and things.

Again, this is consistent with the concept of report-talk as opposed to rapport-talk.

- They tend to use more mechanisms for controlling the topic of a conversation and problem-solving, in line with their goals or objectives. For instance, when they hear a complaint, they see it as a challenge to find a solution.

While I can think of individual men and women who don't correspond neatly to these norms – and even contradict them – I see the patterns of gender difference play out repeatedly in groups and communities. I worked in one organization where the members of a senior team discussed how they were going to work together and made a commitment to support each other on a one-to-one basis. A month or two later, we met to review progress. The men thought it was going great, but the women weren't so sure. It turned out that their interpretations of what it meant to be supportive were very different. The men had made diligent efforts to do a rapid daily check-in while travelling home, which is characteristic of report-talk. The women were disappointed by this. They'd hoped to share the burden of each other's frustrations and concerns in a way that was more consistent with rapport-talk. When the pressure was on, they felt it was a case of 'every man for himself'.

COMMUNICATE LIKE A MAN

Maya has a new role as divisional head of marketing for a consumer-products business. There are very few women at her level. She has a French boss called Lukas who's based in Hong Kong and they're sitting down for Maya's annual review. Lukas has personally selected Maya for his team, and he is full of praise for her. She has a difficult job which requires developing marketing campaigns across multiple countries. This is what happens when they get onto the topic of Maya's personal development:

Maya, as you work in a functional role, the key to success will be how you negotiate and get your voice heard across the business lines.

Yes, I can see that.

In my view, your biggest development area is in being a resolute leader. When someone challenges you, you tend to show flexibility rather than being definitive. You need to be able to say, 'I hear what you're saying and I disagree with your position.'

OK.

It's about being assertive and standing up to people. Being resolute is the archetype of a warrior, and I'd like to see it coming out in you more. You'll have an opportunity to test this by fighting for the budget you need.

Lukas is genuinely trying to support Maya. He knows that some of her peers are forthright characters and wants her to hold her ground with them. What he doesn't realize is that he's effectively saying, 'You need to respond in these situations more like a man.'

Maya is now in a tricky place. Her success has been built on her ability to collaborate and, when she's at her best, she's able to discuss and generate ideas with others, arriving at a collective view that she couldn't have reached on her own. But she's also keen to take on Lukas's feedback, and it's not long before she gets an opportunity. She's in a meeting where a local marketing manager has a difference of opinion with her, so she draws on her warrior archetype and says in a very forthright tone, 'No, this is how it needs to be.' It goes down badly, partly because it's an out-of-character response, but also because the manager feels that he's received a public put-down in front of his colleagues and it has an impact, in his mind at least, on his status.

After their confrontation, Maya resolves any differences offline with the marketing manager, but it leaves her with the same question – only intensified – regarding how she can find her own voice. Over the course of the following year, she comes to the conclusion that the language of being a warrior isn't helpful, because it has connotations in her mind with brute force. Returning to the distinction between power and authority, power can flow in any direction, and Maya has more of it than many of her colleagues because she's built strong relationships across the business. If she uses her power wisely, she's perfectly able to stand up for herself in front of her peers or someone who's in a higher position of authority. She can also be direct when the situation calls for it, but she needs to do so in her own style, without compromising her values. She can draw on her ability to ask questions that test and sharpen the thinking of her colleagues, rather than being prescriptive.

WHAT TO DO?

STEP 1:
Talk About Differences

When Lukas says that Maya needs to develop her warrior archetype, he is trying to help her succeed, and it doesn't occur to him that he may be creating an internal conflict for her. He wants to foster her self-expression but he inadvertently quashes it. Similar situations occur countless times each day in our workplaces, creating Mixed Messages and leaving people in the Bad Place, even though the other person's intentions are perfectly sound.

If Maya and Lukas recognize the role that gender can play in conversation, they can discuss the challenges and opportunities that it throws up:

As there are few women at your level, what challenges does this create for you?

For starters, I find meetings and conference calls very frustrating. The conversations are highly competitive and it can feel as if nobody's listening. I'm reluctant to barge my way in, so I don't always speak up.

It's a good observation. I'm not sure we're even aware that we do this.

At other times I find myself saying things for the sake of it, to get my voice heard, because I don't want to be seen as a wallflower. I don't like doing this, because I'm speaking for the wrong reason.

I think we'd benefit from resetting our agreements on how we talk together. We've certainly strayed into bad habits.

There is learning for both Maya and Lukas in this conversation. By understanding that competing for status is part of the male ritual, Maya can see that her male counterparts aren't intending to be inconsiderate and rude. Even so, she needs to be willing to elbow her way into a discussion if she has a point to make. She doesn't need to dominate it, but she can't expect everyone else to wait for her either.

For his part, Lukas can do more to ensure his meetings don't devolve into Dominatricks. Since the loudest voice isn't necessarily the wisest or the most considered one, he can encourage the contribution of people who don't want to fight to be heard. This applies to Maya, but by no means exclusively, because the more reflective men on Lukas's team have the same complaint. Lukas could solve the problem by following the centuries-old tradition of Native American council meetings, in which the sacred power of words was granted to the person holding the 'talking stick', and everyone else had to wait their turn to talk. This practice forced slow listening and prevented people from firing off opinions while a speaker was mid-sentence. As the talking stick was being passed to you, you had a few precious seconds to engage your rational brain, increasing the chances that you'd speak mindfully. Once the principle of respecting each other's speaking is instilled into the culture of any team, the stick is no longer required.

Lukas can also welcome the fact that women will ask more questions. It has been reported that 72 per cent of men say that women ask *too many* questions, and this is an example of how we can draw judgements about each other rather than recognizing and valuing differences.[7] If Lukas and his team can learn to encourage more questions, their conversations will become richer and their thinking will be more rigorous. And if they can listen slowly instead of Skimming each other's sentences, they'll avoid speaking over each other.

Talk to the people you work with about the way that you conduct conversation. Gender is by no means the only factor in the equation, but it's probably the least discussed. Some people are reluctant to talk about gender differences due to the fear of appearing to be prejudiced, but doing so in a spirit of curiosity can allow you to raise awareness and appreciate each other's respective contribution.

STEP 2:
Balance Opposites

Leaders and managers often recruit people in their own image, even if they do so unconsciously, on the basis that homogeneity leads to a more convivial working environment. But, in doing so, there's a risk that they are promoting narrow-mindedness.

The solution is to encourage diversity and then challenge yourself to bring the best out in people. If you manage a team, a rich and healthy dynamic is created when you can bring together people who are reflective and extroverted, competitive and team oriented, male and female. Whatever the ratio for your own workplace, it's vital to place a high value on people who represent the minority so they don't get sidelined. If your team is highly action oriented, the most important person to your success may be the one who asks questions, raises concerns and takes a more reflective stance.

Whether your working environment is predominantly male or female, the same principle applies when it comes to gender. Maya has something to contribute that's largely invisible to Lukas and her other male colleagues because report-talk is the water that they swim in. The truth is that we desperately need both rapport-talk and report-talk.

Lesson 12: Encourage differences, not conformity.

Chapter 13

DEMAND Clarity

HOW TO AVOID CROSSED WIRES IN CONVERSATION

Many years ago, I was involved in a minor car crash. The other driver was at fault and admitted liability. He was paying privately for the repair work, and we took the car to Fabio, a mechanic who owned a small garage. After the work had been completed and paid for, we found that water was leaking into the back of our car. Since the claim had been settled, and Fabio was now shrugging his shoulders, we became exasperated. Finally my wife Sally decided to call Fabio one Saturday morning and had a difficult and very direct conversation with him.

After putting the phone down, Sally said that Fabio was 'getting his people to look into it' and remarked that his Italian accent sounded far stronger than usual. A panic followed when it dawned on me that I had the contact details for two Fabios in my phone. Far from running a small car-repair workshop in north London, the Fabio whom Sally had spoken to was the European managing director of a company with subsidiaries in 35 countries and revenues of over €100 million. He lived in a European ski resort and flew his own plane to work. Not only had Sally called him at the weekend, but she had informed him that his attitude was disappointing, his workmanship was shabby and his integrity was questionable.

A stream of apologies followed the mix-up. Fabio was very forgiving, and Sally and I were able to see the funny side of it after about 10 years.

The problems of crossed wires are bad enough when we speak the same language, but the possibilities for confusion go up exponentially when translation is required. In Wales, road signs are typically in both Welsh and English, and new signs in Swansea need to be signed off by the council translation department. Looking to block access for heavy vehicles near to a supermarket, a local authority official sent an email requesting translation for: 'No entry for heavy goods vehicles. Residential site only'. This reply came back almost instantaneously: *'Nid wyf yn y swyddfa ar hyn o bryd. Anfonwch unrhyw waith i'w gyfieithu'*.[1] Delighted at such a speedy response, the council had the sign manufactured and erected, only to be contacted by local residents asking why it read: 'I am not in the office at the moment. Send any work to be translated.' An autoreply message had been taken for a translation.

Mind you, they got away lightly compared to the ad-agency copywriter whose commercial should have asked, 'Got milk?' but instead asked Mexican women, 'Are you lactating?' There could have been riots in Mexico when 'It takes a tough man to make a tender chicken' was translated as 'It takes a virile man to make a chicken pregnant.' And Ford Motor Company bosses sought to woo customers in Belgium with an ad that read, 'Every car has a high-quality body', only to find that it translated as 'Every car has a high-quality corpse.' Compared to these muck-ups, the road sign in Swansea was a minor blemish.

CLOSE THE LOOP

Unfortunately the consequences of Mixed Messages can be catastrophic. The deadliest accident in aviation history occurred on 27 March 1977 at Los Rodeos Airport in Tenerife when a conspiracy of events and a series of crossed wires caused two Boeing 747s to collide on the runway. Both planes had been bound for Las Palmas in Gran Canaria but diverted mid-flight to the smaller airport of Tenerife after a bomb exploded in the Las Palmas airport passenger terminal. As it was a Sunday, only two traffic controllers were on duty in the Tenerife control tower and they must have cursed their luck as the airport filled with parked planes. When the taxiway became blocked, the only solution was for planes to taxi *and* take off on the same runway.

As flights were cleared to take off again, the fog rolled in across Tenerife airport. The traffic controllers could see nothing from the control tower and, since they had no ground radar, they relied entirely on radio communication with the pilots. Shortly after 5pm, two Boeing 747s faced each other a kilometre apart on the same stretch of runway. The instruction was for Pan Am Flight 1736 to taxi partway up the runway to the third exit, allowing KLM Flight 4805 to hurtle down the runway and take off.

The black-box transcripts make for grim reading, but reveal the difference between an 'open-loop' and a 'closed-loop' conversation.[2] In short, an open-loop conversation leaves room for doubt, while a closed loop ensures that all parties are on the same wavelength. While the Pan Am plane was taxiing, the air traffic controller asked the co-pilot to take the third intersection off the runway:

Taxi into the runway and, ah, leave the runway third, third on your left.

Third to the left, OK.

But the accent of the local ground controller was strong and there was still an element of doubt, evidenced by this conversation in the cockpit between the flight engineer, the captain and the co-pilot:

Third, he said.

I think he said first.

I'll ask him again.

The loop hadn't been closed, so they went back again, this time speaking to the other controller and asking him to confirm whether they should turn left at the third intersection. The controller replied:

The third one, sir. One, two, three. Third. Third one.

To make utterly sure that they had all heard correctly this time, the crew closed the loop amongst themselves:

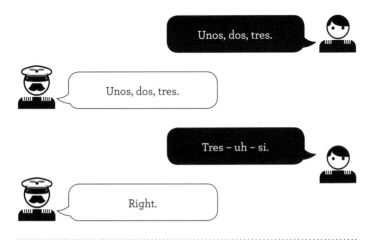

Unos, dos, tres.

Unos, dos, tres.

Tres – uh – si.

Right.

THE COST OF MIXED MESSAGES

As it happened, the plane missed the third intersection, most probably due to poor signage and fog, with visibility down to around 100 metres according to witnesses. The Pan Am crew informed traffic control that they were taxiing to the fourth intersection. Meanwhile, further up the runway, the KLM crew contacted the control tower to confirm that they were ready to take off:

We are now at take-off.

OK [pause], stand by for take-off. I will call you.

After listening to the black-box recordings dozens of times, accident investigators couldn't agree whether the message from KLM 4805 was 'We are now at take-off' or 'We are now uh takin' off.' Either way, the words were hurried and we must remember that the first language for the ground controllers was Spanish; for the KLM crew it was Dutch, and for the Pan Am crew it was English. In a long chain of contributory events, this was a crucial moment. The controller believed he'd given the captain of the KLM plane a clear message to stand by for further instructions. Meanwhile the captain took 'OK' to mean that clearance had been given. In the aftermath of the crash, a debate raged over the use of the word 'OK'. We don't know exactly what part it played, but it's a reminder never to underestimate the power of language and the potential for Mixed Messages.

The lesson from the ensuing tragedy was that the flight controllers and both sets of cabin crews were in an open-loop conversation. Rather than closing the loop, the KLM captain released the brakes and began to initiate the take-off process. As he did so, his flight engineer overheard this message from the Pam Am plane:

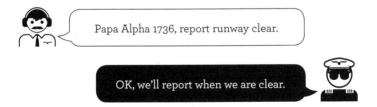

Papa Alpha 1736, report runway clear.

OK, we'll report when we are clear.

When he heard this last comment, alarm bells rang in the head of the flight engineer on the KLM flight. Fearing that the Pan Am flight was still on the runway, and running out of time to abort take-off, he made a last-ditch effort to close the loop with his colleagues in the cockpit. Both the co-pilot and the captain were unanimous in their response:

Is he not clear then?

What did you say?

Is he not clear, that Pan American?

Oh, yes [emphatically].

At this point, the KLM plane was accelerating and the pilot's attention was fully focused on taking off. He was one of the most highly respected KLM captains, and it's very possible that his authority and experience led the flight engineer to assume that his superior couldn't be wrong. But 20 seconds after the flight engineer queried whether the runway was clear, the planes collided. Of 248 passengers and crew on the KLM flight, there were no survivors. On the Pan Am flight, 335 out of 396 people on board were killed.[3]

Time pressures often play a part in Mixed Messages, and this was no exception. The KLM crew were at risk of running over their allocated duty hours. They needed to get their passengers to Las Palmas, pick up travellers who'd been hanging around there for six hours, and then fly back to Amsterdam before they breached duty time regulations. It's a horrible fact that one extra question could have avoided such a tragedy. If the KLM crew had asked, 'Please confirm, is the runway clear for take off?' the presence of the Pan Am plane on the runway would have been corroborated.

THE ROLE OF INFERENCE AND ASSUMPTION

When we're reading text, we usually have the opportunity to read it as many times as we wish, but conversation presents a real challenge because our words are fleeting. When you study transcripts of conversations, it becomes apparent how often we shift direction, fail to finish sentences or jump from one idea to the next. To help us along, we skim people's sentences and use inferences to fill in missing information that isn't explicitly stated by the speaker. An inference is a mental step, in which we conclude that something is true in light of something else being true, or at least appearing to be true.

How does this work in practice? When the captain of KLM Flight 4805 believed he had been given clearance to take off, he assumed that the Pan Am plane *wasn't* any longer on the runway. By contrast, when the KLM flight engineer overheard the Pan Am message saying, 'OK, we'll report when we are clear', he inferred that the plane *was* still on the runway, prompting him to question his pilot and co-pilot. It's for exactly this reason that we need to close the loop by checking with each other.

These situations happen every day, although rarely with so much at stake. Guy Goma, a young graduate from the Congo, accidentally became an instant celebrity when he turned up at the BBC for a job interview as a technical data cleanser. Mistaken in the reception area for an online music expert with the same first name, the bewildered young graduate found himself being rushed into the make-up department and led onto a live set, where he was interviewed by the BBC consumer affairs correspondent about a trademark dispute between Apple Corps and Apple Computer. The look of horror on his face is priceless television.

How did this mix-up happen? When the producer asked, 'Are you Guy?' and got 'Yes' in reply, he inferred the man in front of him was Guy Kewney. As for Guy Goma, he assumed that the situation was an unexpected part of his job interview and therefore didn't ask if there'd been a mix-up. What's the lesson here? Inferences and assumptions can happen so quickly and automatically that we have little choice in the moment as to whether we make them, but we do have the opportunity to check them.

WHAT TO DO?

STEP 1:
Check You're On the Same Page

Closing the loop requires double-checking your understanding . For example, construction manager Sai's last job involved building a huge office block in London. It's standard practice to use steel props to support temporary structures while the floors are being built and, once they're no longer load-bearing, the props can be dismantled. A new supervisor had arrived on site and, although he'd obtained the necessary permit, he was Spinning from one activity to the next and mistakenly wrote the wrong floor number on the task sheet that he handed to Nathan and Josh, who were removing the steelwork. Having gone to the tenth floor as instructed, Nathan wanted to get on with the job; this was their conversation:

Right, these must be the ones.

Are you sure? I thought the temporary props were on the ninth floor. And they should be painted green.

It's got tenth floor written on the task sheet.
Let's get on with it.

Look, you're probably right, but I want to check.

Nathan was irritated at the delay, but Josh did exactly the right thing by stopping the job and calling his supervisor so that he could close the loop. It turned out that Nathan and Josh were minutes away from striking the props under a 200-ton mobile crane, which could have crashed onto the streets of London from the tenth floor. Sai learned a huge lesson from this narrow escape; his men always need to close the loop.

Civil servant Finn also experiences a painful misunderstanding. A document states that the cost of introducing a new national policy will be £36 million. This number is included in an information pack for the minister of education. The person who produces the document is too busy Spinning to notice that he's made a typing error –the correct number is actually £63 million – and they narrowly avoid the minister quoting the wrong figure during a radio interview. Although it isn't actually Finn's fault, his department is in the doghouse.

Smaller examples of Mixed Messages occur all the time in our workplaces and can so easily be avoided. This requires nothing other than checking. In Josh's case, he called his supervisor, Mike:

Hi Mike. I know our task sheet says that we're striking props on the tenth floor, but I want to make 100 per cent sure these aren't props for the crane.

 Tenth floor? No, it's the ninth floor.

Well it says the tenth floor on the paperwork.

 Don't move. I'm coming up now. I think you're on the wrong floor.

STEP 2:
Check Accountabilities and Actions

Start your meetings by reviewing progress on any outstanding commitments, without indulging in the story of why something did or didn't happen. If you keep these conversations sharp, you'll create a culture of accountability in which people honour their word.

Don't tolerate conversations or meetings where you go away with fuzzy actions; otherwise everything you've discussed is likely to be wasted. A simple practice is to stop the meeting 10 minutes before the end instead of trying to cram a couple more topics into your remaining time. Now identify and write down what actions need to be taken, who is accountable for each one and when they need to be completed. As the proverb goes, the palest ink is better than the best memory.

Lesson 13: Prevent problems later by getting clarity now.

Chapter

NEGOTIATE
Agreements

HOW TO GET YOUR NEEDS MET, AND THEIRS

In 1912, Milunka Savić was a young Serbian woman whose brother was called up to serve in the first Balkan War. Not wanting to miss out on the action, 24-year-old Milunka cropped her hair and signed up too. Having proved her valour at the Battle of Bregalnica in 1913, she was decorated and promoted to corporal. It was only in the second Balkan War, when she was severely wounded, that field surgeons discovered their patient was a woman.

This led to an awkward conversation between Milunka and her commanding officer, who announced that Milunka would be transferring to the Nursing Corp. Not surprisingly, she wasn't best pleased with this idea and argued her case to resume the post she'd already excelled in. Caught in two minds, the commanding officer said he would take some time to think about it. Sensing he had wobbled, Milunka promptly took the upper hand in the negotiation. 'I will wait,' she said.

After she'd stood to attention for an hour, the commanding officer caved in, and Milunka went back to work. Once there, she rewarded his trust with her bravery. By the end of World War I, her medal collection would make the strongest shelf buckle under its weight. Serbia awarded her its coveted Order of the Star of Karađorđe (twice); Russia, the Cross of St George; and Britain, the Most Distinguished Order of St Michael. France gave her the Légion d'Honneur (twice) and topped it off with the Croix de Guerre.

So what are the essential principles of effective negotiation?

THINK LIKE A NEGOTIATOR

When I had my first job in India I remember my employer saying that he rarely paid full price for a pair of shoes in the UK. I was rather shocked at this idea. I could barter on a street corner in

Rajasthan, but surely not in the high street in Britain? I realized that he and I saw life in very different ways; everything for him was an opportunity to negotiate, and a price tag was merely a starting point for a conversation. I had much to learn.

When you think about it, you negotiate on a daily basis. If you have young children, you'll wrangle over bedtimes and treats. If you have teenagers, you'll argue over boundaries. If you have an exacting boss, you'll need to push back on his or her demands. Whether you're a soft touch or haggle to the death, each of these situations involves negotiation, and getting the balance right isn't easy. If you say 'no' to everything, people will decide you're obstructive and won't have any time for you. If you're a sucker for saying 'yes', you'll sink under the weight of promises you can't deliver. When you start viewing yourself as a negotiator, life offers endless opportunities to practise.

THE RELATIONSHIP COMES FIRST

Ria's telecoms company shares the cost of installing and maintaining its mobile network with a competitor. This is a common practice in her industry and makes great commercial sense, but it means that Ria and her counterparts have a schizophrenic relationship; they are partners in relation to their infrastructure and competitors in relation to their customers. To complicate things, their organizations have different strategies. Ria's company wants to roll out a new network as swiftly as possible but its joint-venture partner can't invest at the same speed. Competing priorities are creating tension, and it feels as though every conversation becomes a source of disagreement and a basis for negotiation. Ria knows they're in the Bad Place when their commercial managers take a copy of the legal contract to meetings.

Up to now Ria and her colleagues have been reluctant to be open and honest with their counterparts because they don't want to lose their negotiating levers. They think that honesty leads to vulnerability, so their conversations are guarded and cagey. After a joint-venture meeting, they typically have an internal debrief in which they look for hidden agendas and discuss how to maintain their advantage. A Blamestorming conversation will go like this:

So what did you make of Robin's rollout plan?

It's quite obvious he's stalling. He's been told to slow everything down.

Did you see his body language when he said it?

Yeah, he was on the defensive from the first minute.

Somehow the leaders on both sides have forgotten that their contract is worth nothing if they have insufficient trust to make it succeed. They are making huge commercial outlays and yet they haven't invested in their relationship. As the German Chancellor Angela Merkel remarked when the political leaders of the Eurozone countries struggled to reach agreement on an economic rescue package for Greece: 'The most important currency has been lost, and that is trust.' This is true in any aspect of life. If Ria and her fellow directors can remember that negotiations always happen with people, and not with nebulous entities such as 'organizations', they may decide to be more honest and open with their counterparts.

KEEP THE BIGGER AIM IN MIND

Both companies in the joint venture have just signed a partnership agreement for the next phase of the network rollout. Their respective lawyers have spent weeks arguing over minor contract clauses relating to liquidated damages that are unlikely ever to be invoked. While they debate small points of principle, the delay to the network rollout has already cost over a million pounds in lost income. The lawyers are reluctant to concede any ground, but each time they fight an individual battle, their relationship receives another dent.

Ria calls a meeting between the leaders on both sides to see if they can find a way forward. She states quite openly that the relationship isn't working and acknowledges that she and her team aren't blameless in the matter. This is the first time she's let her guard down but it allows others to be honest too. There's a gradual realization that they've become more invested in being right than in keeping sight of the bigger picture. As one of them puts it, they're practically arguing over who'll pick up the drinks bill at the bar. Now Ria asks everyone:

> If we were one company, how would we go about building a mobile network?

This opens up a conversation about what's possible and what's needed, instead of what's wrong. Self-righteousness gives way to curiosity, and they rediscover the ambition that had initially brought the two organizations together. In a single day, they make more progress in their relationship than in the previous three years. There will always be some conflicting requirements and bumps in the road, but at least they're discussing them within the context of a shared aspiration. They decide to meet every quarter to have a similar conversation. This is a wise move, and holds true in any relationship: if you spend too much time arguing over small issues, you'll lose sight of the possibility that brought you together in the first place.

WHAT TO DO?

STEP 1:
Prepare Thoroughly

Finn's friend works for a consulting company that has several government contracts and they're recruiting for the role of policy adviser. Finn puts himself forward and comes across well enough to be asked back again. Toward the end of the second interview, they discuss more practical questions:

I'm afraid it's a fact of life in the consulting industry that we need to go where the clients are. Are you prepared to travel?

Yes, that's fine with me.

As for salary, you'd be starting on £34,000 and there's a profit-sharing scheme that you'd benefit from if we have a successful year.

Right, that sounds great.

Lastly, holiday allowance would start at four weeks. After three years' service it goes up to five weeks. Do you have any other questions about terms or pay, if we were to offer you the role?

No, I think that's it, thank you. I'll wait to hear from you.

It's only later that Finn worries about how much travel would be involved, given that he's getting married in the next year and is keen to avoid work Spilling into his home life. He also questions why he'd be paid £34,000 when the job description says '£32,000 to £40,000'. Since he didn't address this in the interview, he feels he's missed his opportunity to ask for a higher salary. Finn was prepared for the questions about his experience and skills, but not for a negotiation.

If he could rewind the interview, Finn would do as much research as possible in advance, gathering background information on his prospective employer and investigating whether other consulting firms are advertising for a similar position. When he finds an advert for a roughly equivalent role with a salary of £38,000, he decides to fill out an application even though the role isn't quite so well suited to his skills. It won't do any harm to have applied for a better-paid role, and it gives him a yardstick for salary-related discussions.

STEP 2:
Understand Your Parameters and Thresholds

If he can figure out his parameters and thresholds in advance, Finn will know when to negotiate and when to walk away. His parameters include salary, working location, accountabilities and promotion prospects. For each of these, he needs to know his preferred outcome and his walkaway points, enabling him to have a different conversation. For example, he can clearly state his position regarding working away from home:

I'm afraid it's a fact of life in the consulting industry that we need to go where the clients are. Are you prepared to travel?

Yes, of course. I'm happy to be away for two nights a week on a regular basis, and occasionally all week, but I wouldn't want this to become the norm.

Since you'd be a policy adviser, you'd be focusing on our government contracts in London and Bristol. If this is the case, you'd have plenty of flexibility, but I can't make any promises in the long term.

This is as much certainty as Finn can hope for, and he feels better for having raised it. By understanding your parameters and thresholds, you'll be more confident and increase the odds of being successful.

STEP 3:
Set an Anchor

While a salary of £34,000 would meet Finn's threshold, he'd be happier if he could negotiate a higher figure, and it will help if he understands the principle of anchoring. If you can put down a marker in the other person's mind, you're likely to negotiate up or down from that point. The anchor needs to be stretching but not absurd, otherwise you'll blow your credibility. This reminds me of an episode of *The Apprentice* in which Philip, a would-be entrepreneur, pitches for a catering contract. He opens the negotiation with a ludicrous price of £65 per head for a selection of canapés, which is met with disdain. Realizing his error, Philip fiddles on his calculator before suggesting 'around £35' per head. When this is dismissed, he blows through his cheeks and asks in a tone of desperation, 'Right, so if we went down to something like £17.50 a head?' Finally they agree on £15, and when the client asks what they'll get for their money, Philip reels off the same menu as at the £65 price tag. Back in the boardroom, Lord Sugar is withering in his assessment. 'You looked like a spiv,' he says. Philip's lesson in negotiation is complete.

If Finn has prepared, the salary conversation could go like this:

As for salary, you'd be starting on £34,000 and there's a profit-sharing scheme that you'd benefit from if we have a successful year.

I've got another application that I've filled out for a similar role, and it's advertising for £38,000, so I'm looking for something closer to that salary.

Well, we can certainly discuss it further. I don't think we'd have room to go that far, but perhaps we could get closer to it.

Finn's done well here. His target salary is actually £35,000 but he puts down an anchor at £38,000 because he knows, unlike Philip on *The Apprentice*, that this is a realistic aim. In the end, the consulting firm offers him £37,000.

STEP 4:
Say No and Make Counter-Offers

Without question, you'll suffer from Stacking, Spinning, Skimming and Spilling if you can't say 'no'. Some people consider it a sign of weakness to decline a request, but this philosophy makes no sense if you end up failing to deliver. Since the person making the request often has no idea how many other commitments you're juggling, or the exact timeframes involved, it's a sign of strength to negotiate appropriate deadlines.

Let's begin with a situation that happens every day – the last five minutes of a meeting. When headteacher Matt meets with his department heads on a Thursday afternoon, he starts to discuss actions and accountabilities as people are packing up:

> Right, let's agree what needs to happen. Lois, can you pick up the proposal for the science trips? I'll need it first thing on Monday.

In the past, Lois would have said 'yes' and then worked on it for half her weekend, even though Matt has given her insufficient notice. This time, she isn't going to make the same mistake:

> What needs to be done?

I just need a description of each of the trips and a breakdown of costs.

 I've got no time to work on it tomorrow, so I can send you a document without the costs by lunchtime on Monday or with the costs by the same time on Tuesday.

Lunchtime on Tuesday will be fine, as long as it's no later. I need to send a briefing pack to the governors on Wednesday.

By suggesting 'first thing on Monday', Matt is only trying to build some contingency into the process. Unless Lois pushes back, he'll be unaware that he's crashing her weekend.

Sometimes you need to weigh one commitment against another. If your boss asks you to deliver something by the end of today, when you're already working flat-out to deliver another project, you need to ask, 'Which of these deadlines is more important?' This gives some of the responsibility back to him or her to make a choice. In the same way, if two people more senior than you make an urgent request, you need to ask them to resolve with each other whose commitment takes precedence. Either way, accepting every request is not sustainable. As the saying goes, don't negotiate out of fear, but don't fear to negotiate either.

Lesson 14: You're a negotiator, whether you like it or not.

Chapter 15

CONSIDER Cultural INFLUENCES

HOW TO TALK ACROSS BORDERS

Many years ago, I worked in Madrid for the first time. I was running a two-day leadership programme for about 40 people, with English-Spanish translation. Knowing we had a huge amount to cover, I was relying on a prompt 9am start, but most people strolled in around 10 minutes late, only to head off in search of coffee. Having finally rounded everyone up and got proceedings underway, they insisted that we stop for another coffee at 11am. I stared nervously at my agenda during the break while the hotel staff served portions of Spanish omelette.

After herding everyone in again, we made decent progress until 2pm, at which point we were called for lunch. I was hoping it would be a smash-and-grab affair, only to find that the restaurant had prepared a three-course meal and the wine bottles had already been uncorked. By 3:30pm, while everyone was enjoying yet more coffee, I was close to desperation, but my Spanish host took me to one side and assured me that the meeting was going splendidly. What followed was a revelation. People were more than happy to work into the evening before heading out for dinner. I realized that, far from being an intrusion, meals were an integral part of their working day and provided an opportunity for conversation. On the second day, I was a reformed man, calling for more omelette at the 11am break. Having embraced this new approach, I flew on to Munich where – compared to my punctilious German hosts who ran everything with impeccable timing – I came across as maddeningly Spanish.

As I travelled further afield, I kept bumping up against my own narrow views about how things ought to be done. I learned, as many global organizations have done to their cost, that it was unreasonable and disrespectful to pitch up in a foreign country and impose my customs on their culture.

LESSONS FROM BEIJING

Project manager Rafa's organization is outsourcing some of its IT development work to China, and Rafa has been tasked with overseeing its delivery, but he experiences a bewildering initiation into Chinese customs. When Rafa sends an email proposing a trip to Beijing in eight weeks' time, he doesn't get a reply from his Chinese counterpart. And when he finally reaches Liu Wei by phone, he can't seem to pin down a meeting date. Each time he pushes for clarity, he gets an obtuse reply:

I'm coming out on the 27th of March. Can we meet at 11am on the 28th?

I'm sure we can.

 OK, so that's confirmed then, is it?

We'll do our best to meet you then.

It's only after his first visit that Rafa realizes Liu Wei means

Call me personally two or three days before you come to Beijing, and we can firm up a broad plan. Then contact me the day before and we'll finalize everything. And remind me on the morning of the meeting that you are coming.

Keeping his diary open allows Liu Wei to stay flexible in case a request comes in from his CEO or a bigger customer. This last-minute approach is normal practice in China, and even the government only announces public holidays with a few days to spare. After a while, Rafa learns to say this:

> I'm arriving in Beijing on the 27th of March and have to leave on the evening of the 30th. I hope that you and your colleagues will be available to meet.

By remaining flexible and using the word 'hope' rather than 'expect', Rafa affirms that their relationship is based on respect rather than control. In China, the secret to successful conversation always lies in being able to read between the lines. While Rafa can sometimes cause offence by missing these subtle cues, confusion can be caused in reverse when Liu Wei and his colleagues assume a subtext even though none is intended.

When he first meets with Liu Wei and his colleagues, Rafa has another cultural wake-up call. They enter the meeting room, and Rafa's in the process of sitting down at the nearest seat by the door when he realizes that there's a commotion. Liu Wei almost shouts in alarm, and ushers an embarrassed Rafa into the seat on the left of his boss, who *faces* the door and is the most senior person present. Liu Wei then sits to the right of his boss. The most junior person sits with his back to the door. There are eight chairs in all – an auspicious number.

To start with, Rafa feels as if Liu Wei is reluctant to get down to business. Every time he brings the conversation back to a discussion about commercial terms or technical requirements, Liu Wei diverts it. After a dinner and a meeting Rafa doesn't feel any further forward, but he's failed to appreciate that, from a Chinese perspective, things are going just fine. Nothing will happen until the foundations of their relationship have been firmly established and this requires patience, which isn't in Rafa's nature. Some of his British and American colleagues are driven to distraction by what they see as an unwillingness to cut out the prevarication. However, for Liu Wei and his colleagues, the process of relationship-building has nothing to do with prevarication; it is a condition for doing business and, if you don't like it, they will partner with another company instead.[1]

YES, YES, YES

Ria's telecoms business has outsourced a significant proportion of its IT operations to India, and Ria – like Rafa in China – is going through a steep cultural learning curve. To start with, she is impressed that the leaders of the Indian software house are supremely confident they can deliver on her requirements. Every request is met with the same response: 'yes'. But over time, some problems start to arise. For example, when Lara in the marketing department in Ria's company creates a new mobile price tariff which offers 1GB of data, 200 minutes of voice time and 500 texts, this message gets relayed over to the software team in India, led by Rahim. As always, the marketing team want it at short notice, and are delighted to find that it's delivered promptly. But when they subsequently want a minor change, this is what happens:

It's pretty straightforward. All we need to do is change the price to £18.99. Everything else stays the same. The guys need it for tomorrow, so can you make this a priority?

I'm afraid it's not so easy as that.

What do you mean?

Well, we didn't build it in that way, so we'll need to rewrite the code. It'll take longer.

The problem can be traced back to the original set of requirements. Rahim assumed that his team was being asked to write a one-off piece of code, and therefore didn't build in components to allow for quick and easy changes. If he had concerns at the time, he didn't raise them. Ria's experience isn't uncommon. Studies of outsourcing relationships between American and western European firms with Indian joint-venture partners have found that many Indian employees are reluctant to voice criticism in face-to-face meetings. One study revealed that they would sometimes email their opinions after the meetings, but this was frustrating for their British counterparts, who wanted discussions to develop ideas, challenge assumptions and express concerns. The conclusion of the study was that, culturally speaking, the desire to please can override the willingness to be assertive, especially in front of authority figures.[2]

DIRECT AND INDIRECT

When head of marketing Maya goes to New York and shows her US colleagues the latest TV adverts for their washing detergent that are broadcasting in the UK, they laugh out loud and can barely believe how abstruse it is. The advert involves a talking bear in a laundrette, with an oblique reference to the product, and it's going down a storm in the UK, where it's part of a long-term strategy to differentiate their offering in a crowded marketplace. In contrast, the latest US advert is about comparison marketing, highlighting how their product is better value than its nearest competitors.

This has parallels with conversational styles in the US and UK. Again, it would be wrong to make universal statements about differences but British conversation often relies on self-deprecating humour, indirectness, deflection and heavy use of irony, all of which can be lost on our American partners, who wonder why on earth we don't just get to the damned point.

I was interviewed on an American radio show shortly after the publication of *Blamestorming*. It's never easy to speak down a phone line on a live broadcast, but I did my utmost to listen, engage truthfully and respond to the questions thrown at me. Afterwards I concluded that, for all my shortcomings, I'd given it my best shot, and sent a recording of the interview to my publicist in the US. He acknowledged my efforts but said, 'The only problem is that you didn't promote your book!' To be honest, I thought I had, but we had a different understanding of what this meant. In my world, it meant making occasional references to my book so that I didn't come across as overly pushy. In his mind, it meant something more upfront. As he rightly said, 'What sounds appropriate – even expected – to a US audience will feel shameless to you.' What feels direct in one culture can be viewed as hedging in another.

WHAT TO DO?

STEP 1:
Think Like a Global Citizen

It would be wholly wrong to imply that everyone from a given country conforms to a set of national traits. Not all Chinese nationals would respond in the same way as Liu Wei, and neither would all Indian nationals display Rahim's desire to please. Besides, countries have strong regional variations. For example, there are well-documented cultural differences between Boston, on the east coast of the USA, and San Francisco on the west coast, even though both cities are politically liberal and have similar economies. Studies by Victoria Plaut, a social and cultural psychologist at the University of California, revealed a strong emphasis on tradition in Boston and on freedom in San Francisco, offering an insight into why cross-regional interactions can go wrong.[3] While these differences are citywide rather than individual, they reinforce the importance of being sensitive to different cultural norms.

In 2009, US politician Newt Gingrich declared, 'I am not a citizen of the world. I think the entire concept is intellectual nonsense and stunningly dangerous.'[4] Whether he likes it or not, our shops are stuffed with products that were grown or built abroad, our personal wealth is tied to the performance of foreign financial markets and, as Bill Gates said, the internet is becoming the town square for the global village of tomorrow. Besides, advances in DNA research have revealed that we're all more closely interconnected than we could have imagined.

Thinking like a global citizen doesn't mean that you have to abandon your national identity and customs, but it requires a willingness to respect and be curious about the norms of other cultures. In practice this means asking how things are done when you're working in that environment. You're not always expected to know; the least you can do is ask.

STEP 2:
Review Your Own Habits

Being curious about the way people communicate in other cultures can provide the spark for self-improvement. For example, I've noticed how my Spanish colleagues turn lunch into a mini-event in their cramped office kitchen. A tablecloth is spread out, giving their meal a dash of personality and a sense of ritual. For half an hour they'll stop Spinning and catch up on each other's lives or discuss the latest rivalries in Spanish football. In doing so, they recreate a practice that has existed for thousands of years in the town square. The positive impact of eating together on collaboration and productivity in the workplace was corroborated by a 15-month study of firefighters in the US, whose job requires them to eat together on site in case they receive an emergency call-out.[5]

Back at work, I observe how my Spanish colleagues communicate with each other in a very straightforward and direct fashion, because the foundations of their relationships are strong. Compared to eating a sandwich at my desk, their informal lunchtime gathering is thoroughly enlightened. The tablecloth is optional, but I've learned that taking a complete break makes my mind sharper and pays dividends for my relationships. Whenever you experience a different culture, you have the chance to review and recalibrate your own working practices.

Lesson 15: Strive to be curious, not to be right.

Chapter 16

GET
Great at
SMALL TALK

HOW SMALL TALK LEADS TO BIG TALK

Between the ages of 6 and 10 months, we develop a form of conversation called babbling, which is the precursor to full-blown language. Since all young children babble, irrespective of where they are born, we know that it's innate rather than learned. As language develops, many parents are subjected to a torrent of talk from their young charges. The story goes that Albert Einstein was quite the opposite and refrained from speaking until he was four, before casually remarking to his dazed parents, 'The soup is too hot!' When they asked why he hadn't talked earlier, young Albert said that everything was in order and he didn't need to. Perhaps this was my first career mistake: rather than blowing my energy on baby-talk, I should have been conserving it for theoretical physics.

Since the publication of *Blamestorming*, I've received more requests by the media to comment on small talk than on any other aspect of conversation. This must be a sign of the times, but it would be a mistake to think it's because most people love small talk. Many of them detest it, seeing it as a necessary evil and an almost criminal waste of time. They connect small talk with fake conversation and would rather have medium talk or big talk.

My question is this: whatever your natural propensity for small talk, why not become an expert in it, for the simple reason that you can? To do so, you have to start looking at small talk as a skill that anyone can develop. I'm not saying that we can all pick up the sense of timing, humour and general love of engaging with others that comes so effortlessly to some people, but we can learn enough to cope with any social situation and even excel at it. Like a Swiss Army knife, small talk can have a multitude of applications in the workplace.

IT'S NOT ABOUT THE WEATHER

I was recently in Greece and noticed that small talk about the weather was a conversation killer. We managed to agree that it was hot, very hot or extremely hot before needing to move to a new topic of discussion. In contrast, we are famous in England for making weather-talk a national pastime. To many foreigners this is unfathomable, but it makes more sense if you realize that we're speaking in code. In other words, when we're discussing our weather, it's not really about the weather.

In her book *Watching the English*, social anthropologist Kate Fox examines the many uses of weather-talk.[1] If you get into a taxi, talking about the weather can be a way of gauging whether the driver is interested in chatting or not. It can also be a straightforward icebreaker, a pause-filler if a conversation gets awkward, or a way to create solidarity by having a mutual moan. In each case, it allows you to make a connection with someone else and establish common ground. For this reason it would be unusual – in England at least – to challenge someone's assessment of the weather conditions, because the point of the interaction is about reciprocity rather than being factually correct.

When teacher Lois meets the parents of a student while shopping, or when entrepreneur Harry has a quick drink in a busy bar with a client, or project manager Rafa bumps into a colleague from the HR department in the canteen, it's not the time or place for big talk. In each situation, small talk allows them to acknowledge and affirm their connection with each other without getting stuck in heavyweight discussion.

CORE PRINCIPLES OF SMALL TALK

So, if reciprocity is the central tenet of small talk, what are the key principles that underpin it?

[1] Show an interest: Whether you like small talk or not, people hugely appreciate it when you show an interest in them. I often ask people to tell me about the best manager they've ever worked for and what he or she actually did to earn their trust and admiration. One man said this, and it stuck in my mind:

> *I worked on a construction project last year where my boss would park every morning at the far end of the site office, next to the back door, so he had to walk past rows of desks en route to his own. He always spent a moment with each person. 'How's Mary?', he would ask his architect, knowing she'd been ill. 'Build it the right way up this time!', he would say to his senior engineer, with a wink. And so on. It might take him 15 minutes to reach his desk, but morale and productivity on site were fantastic: we'd do anything for him. After a while he got called away to another project, and I remember the day our new boss arrived. He parked opposite the front entrance, made a beeline for his office and vanished into meetings. Within a month we all wanted to move to another job.*

Managers who say they don't have time for small talk are missing the point: they're managing people, not cogs in wheels, and they'll receive loyalty to the degree that they create affinity.

[2] Ask questions that invite a fuller response: Thankfully, taking an interest requires nothing more than a willingness to ask questions. I'm always amazed at how the most introverted individuals become so animated when talking about a topic that taps into the underground wells of their interests and passions.

A key factor is the way you phrase your questions. Let's say you ask someone where they live and they say, 'Birmingham'. Then you say, 'Do you like it there?' and they reply, 'It's OK.' At this point you may feel like I did when discussing the weather in Greece. But by slightly changing your question, you can invite a fuller response. For example, there is a subtle but important difference between asking 'How long have you lived in Birmingham?' and 'How did you come to live in Birmingham?' This is the extraordinary thing about language; by changing the emphasis or rephrasing the question, you can take your conversations to a different place.

The best retail assistants understand this point. If I walk into a shop, and a store assistant asks, 'Can I help you?' I will usually say 'No!' as a kind of knee-jerk response. I think this is because I want to feel as if I'm buying something rather than being sold it. In contrast, if I'm asked an open question, rather than a closed one, the conversation is more likely to flourish. I remember going into Nordstrom in New York many years ago, shortly after becoming a father for the first time, and I wandered through the soft-toy area. Rather than asking me if I needed help, the assistant asked me who I was seeking a present for. Within a minute or two, we were discussing daughters, birth weights and sleepless nights. Sportswear-store manager Oona knows this as well as anyone. If she can train her store assistants to ask questions that elicit a deeper response, their customer service is better and their sales are higher.

[3] Take note of details: One boss, who had a large workforce in his factory and couldn't possibly remember all the conversations he had with people, kept a notebook and made a conscious effort after chatting to them to jot down the names of their children or the sports team they followed. If he hadn't seen them for a while, he could seek them out and ask, 'How's Archie's football going?'

You may think this is a bit forced but, if someone has recalled that you make your own pasta or raise money for a particular charity, do you really care whether they've got an amazing memory or a notebook to write things down in? The point is that they've gone out of their way on your behalf. And while most people are too busy Spinning to even remember your name, the people who make the extra effort and make it personal stick out a mile.

Sir Alex Ferguson is regarded as one of the greatest sports managers of all time, having won 38 trophies in 26 years at Manchester United. Ryan Giggs, who spent 23 seasons in the club's first team, said:

> *He had this unbelievable ability to remember everyone's name. He knows Kath on reception, the laundry girls, the chefs and the cleaners. You have 65–70 players, plus the schoolboys, which is another 30 or 40, and he knew them all because he took an interest in what they were doing and how they were progressing.*[2]

Many of us complain that our memory for names is deplorably bad, to the point that we forget someone's name three seconds after being introduced to them. There's a simple physiological reason for this: when we meet someone, our cognitive processes are occupied with making eye contact, saying hello and advancing to shake hands, and therefore we often fail to listen. By simply placing your attention on the person's name, and saying it back to them early on in your conversation, you'll increase the likelihood that you can recall it at a later date. Doing so is a small but significant demonstration that you're taking an interest in their life, which in turn makes small talk easier and more fulfilling.

THE QUEEN'S COUNSEL

Unlike me, my son Marcus has always been happy to chat to anyone, irrespective of their age or rank. I took him to a corporate lunch at a professional rugby match when he was aged 10. I sat on his right and a high-profile lawyer sat on his left. The man was a Queen's Counsel, an accolade awarded for excellence in advocacy in the higher courts of England, and he'd just completed a prosecution case that ran in the national press. The lady on my other side started chatting to me and I became increasingly anxious that I was neglecting Marcus. But each time I looked over to check, he seemed to be locked in conversation with the lawyer. This continued throughout the meal, to the point that I didn't want to interrupt them. Afterwards, I went up to the man to thank him so much for chatting to my son. Giving me a very gracious and slightly wry smile, he said, 'I mainly listened!'

Wonderful as it is to be gregarious, people who can natter to anyone can also improve their skills in small talk. At times they can inadvertently wash people overboard by filling every gap in the conversation and forget that they need to create opportunities for other people to speak. While people who are more reflective may be less inclined to initiate a conversation, it would be wrong to conclude that they don't want to play an equal part in it.

WHAT TO DO?

STEP 1:
Go Out of Your Way to Practise

If you're too busy Stacking and Spinning you probably won't pick up on passing references that can open up new opportunities. Spend a few minutes every day speaking to someone whom you don't know so well, or don't know at all. Through practice, it ceases to be an endurance test and becomes a chance to learn something new.

I once worked with a leader in South Africa whom I'd spoken to on the phone from the UK, but hadn't actually met. After landing in Johannesburg, I travelled straight to his office, where I met him and his deputy. He didn't waste any time on small talk and was keen to crack on with the business of the day, but I felt conscious that I knew almost nothing about either of them, so I asked them to tell me about their background and life outside work. After a moment, the leader said: 'I love sailing. In fact, I've represented my country at the world championships and was in training for the Olympics.' His deputy was incredulous and they were both aghast that, after four years of working together and thousands of conversations, they knew so little about each other. In that moment, small talk led to big talk, and the context for our work that week became clear.

When you think about it, your relationship with your partner and your closest friends probably began with small talk. The same can apply in the workplace. The only reason I worked in India as a teenager was because my mother chatted to another customer in her local butcher's shop in England. Bill Hewlett and Dave Packard met at Stanford University, to which Hewlett only got admitted because of a small-talk conversation. One of the lecturers had informed Hewlett's mother that her son's academic record didn't warrant him being offered a place and asked why he had applied. In reply, she said that her late husband, Walter Hewlett, had studied at the university and Bill wanted to follow in his footsteps. It transpired that the lecturer had taught her husband and rated him as the best student he'd ever had. Young Bill was duly offered a place and met Dave Packard. Thank goodness for mothers who conduct rapport-talk.

STEP 2
Have an Exit Strategy

There's nothing wrong with having an exit strategy if you want to move on from a small-talk conversation. In my view, it's not necessary to come up with a lengthy justification. Glossy magazines are packed with advice on exit lines, and most of them are terrible. Groucho Marx probably came up with the rudest exit line when he said, 'I never forget a face, but in your case I'd be glad to make an exception.' When I want to move on, I tend to take a more British approach and say, 'Glad to meet you', before making my departure.

Lesson 16: You never know where small talk will take you.

Chapter 17

MANAGE
Confrontation

HOW TO MAKE THE DIFFICULT CONVERSATIONS COUNT

As a young boy at school in the 1970s, Formula One Top Trumps was our ultimate game. We traded cards that compared the speed and horsepower of cars on the Grand Prix circuits, but many of the drivers of these cars were no longer alive. In fact, it was part and parcel of the sport that vehicles and drivers would crash and burn while their competitors dodged the wreckage to complete their own race. In his autobiography, Sir Jackie Stewart, three times Formula One World Champion, described the situation like this: 'Imagine an eleven-year window of time when you lose fifty-seven – repeat fifty-seven – friends and colleagues, often watching them die in horrific circumstances doing exactly what you do, weekend after weekend.'[1]

Sick of the unnecessary loss of life, and exasperated with the inertia of racetrack owners and car designers, Stewart decided that enough was enough. When he took up the battle to negotiate better safety standards, critics lined up to take shots at him in the press, claiming he was taking the masculinity out of the sport, and one of his fellow drivers even made chicken noises when he was in earshot.

While writing *Workstorming*, I asked Jackie to comment on this phase in his life, and he began by pointing out that he suffers from extreme dyslexia. Condemned as a boy by his schoolteachers for being stupid, he couldn't read and write like the 'clever folks', as he described them. Instead he developed his communication skills, which served him well when dealing with his detractors:

When I was carrying out my campaign for improved safety,
I was faced with considerable opposition on a global basis.
There were times when I wasn't the most popular racing
driver in the world, simply because I was asking for money

to be spent on something that, in spite of the fatality rate, no one believed was required. In the end we got it done, but it was one of the most hostile successes I have ever achieved.

Jackie emphasized that his accomplishments were built on the ability to build relationships based on respect, integrity and care, rather than animosity. But this isn't easy when you don't see eye to eye. So how can you deal with the really tough conversations, such as a customer being rude, a colleague being provocative, or when you need to give difficult feedback about someone's performance? What's more, how can you clear things up once they've gone wrong?

GET ALONGSIDE PEOPLE

Difficult conversations are part and parcel of Martha's day at the intensive-care unit of her local hospital, where she works as a volunteer. Family members who arrive at the ward are in a state of shock, grief and anxiety. In the reception area, Martha must ask them to wait for the approval of the nurses before visiting a patient, but this is difficult for visitors to understand and they often see her as an obstacle. This morning, Mr Jukes has arrived to see his partner, who has a life-threatening illness:

I'm here to see Lucy Jukes. Can I go in now?

If you could wait here for a moment, I'll go and speak to the nurses.

It's my right to see Lucy now. No one's going to tell me to wait, least of all a receptionist.

Of course it's your right to see her. I realize five minutes feels like an eternity. The reason we ask you to wait is so we can check whether the nurses are in the middle of doing a procedure for Lucy. I'll talk to them immediately and come back to you.

Martha has learned not to react, and this is the first principle of difficult conversations. No matter what someone says, she doesn't take it personally or get embroiled in an argument. Instead, she recognizes that visitors are lashing out at their situation. Martha would be surprised to know that she's following a process similar to the one developed by the FBI's hostage-negotiation unit, and it applies to any disagreement or difficult conversation.[2] The five steps of the model are:

[1] **Listen actively** – make sure the other person knows that you're listening
[2] **Empathize** – understand the person's perspective and feelings
[3] **Establish rapport** – create trust and affinity such that the other person returns your empathy
[4] **Influence** – work on solving the problem with them, now that you've earned their trust
[5] **Change behaviour** – influence them to act in a positive and constructive way.

According to Chris Voss, who was the FBI's chief international hostage negotiator, most people try to start at Step 4 and then wonder why the conversation goes wrong. Voss emphasizes that it's madness to think that emotions don't play a part in difficult conversations. Even if you acknowledge and manage your own feelings, the other person's emotions may be raging, so you can't afford to ignore them. Because Martha listens actively and empathizes with Mr Jukes, he realizes that she's alongside him rather than just enforcing hospital protocol. Later on in the day, Martha brings him a cup of tea and encourages him to find some food, but assures him that she'll be in touch with him instantly if there's a change in Lucy's condition. He's grateful for her assistance, but he especially appreciates her understanding, and even apologizes for his brusque behaviour earlier.

Martha's communication skills are applicable to anyone in a customer-facing role. If a customer has a problem, it's difficult to have a sensible conversation until you've made efforts to get into their world. Think how often you've stood in a long queue in a shop, getting more and more fed up. When you reach the till, an assistant says, 'I'm sorry to keep you waiting', but you get the sense that they've said it a thousand times and aren't really sorry at all. But once in a while, an assistant will say those same words in a different way. They seem genuinely apologetic for the inconvenience and irritation that you feel, and you get the impression that they're alongside you. In an instant, your negative emotions seem to disappear down an invisible plughole. If your staff can communicate in this way, your customers will come back to you forever. Martha's skills are also relevant for every manager. Being delivery focused, negotiating hard and holding people to account for their promises will get you so far. But if you can also listen, empathize and establish rapport, your staff will repay you with their loyalty.

KEEP YOUR CENTRE OF GRAVITY

Head of marketing Maya and her team are presenting their work on a new digital campaign. Her internal client is Jon, who's notoriously direct but seems to get away with it because he's results oriented and has a strong track record. What irritates Maya is his way of putting her team down and engaging in one-upmanship.

On this occasion, Maya rises to his bait:

> I think the campaign's weak. I'm underwhelmed.

> Jon, we were given the brief for this campaign three weeks ago, so you're lucky to get anything at all.

> Well, it shows, that's for sure.

> Now you're being insulting.

A conversation moves into Escalation in the blink of an eye. Maya and Jon both have colleagues in the meeting who can see battle lines being drawn, and their argument won't do anything for cross-company relationships. Stories of bust-ups and head-on collisions will spread within minutes. Here's how Maya can deal with Jon. Each of these strategies will change the direction of their conversation:

[1] **Don't react** – Jon is looking for a reaction, so the best way of dealing with him is not to react. Funnily enough, Maya's more likely

to earn his respect in this way. She may want to challenge him when she has a clearer head but the immediate priority is to avoid a public brawl. If she can keep her centre of gravity in the face of Jon's provocation, they can still have a productive conversation.

[2] **Ask what's needed** – as soon as Maya asks this, she takes the conversation away from Jon's opinions into a more proactive place:

> I think the campaign's weak. I'm underwhelmed.

> OK. So what's needed to get it into better shape? Given the short lead-time, we said we'd be at concept stage by today, so it'll help to understand how we can improve it.

[3] **Press the STOP! button** – if the conversation's escalating, this is your emergency exit. By pressing the STOP! button you create some distance from the other person. You can do this by suggesting that everyone has a quick break or signal that you want to shift topic. In Maya's case, she might tell Jon that she wants to review the campaign requirements with him offline. She can do this in a way that's courteous but firm. Pressing the STOP! button can feel uncomfortable, but it's better than having a bust-up.

SET UP TO SUCCEED

Entrepreneur Harry is on his way out of the office and passes Andy, his head of finance. A few days ago they did a presentation to a private investor to try to raise funds for the next stage of their latest venture:

Hi Andy, I need to catch up with you. We didn't get the funding, I'm afraid.

 Damn. What was the feedback?

 Well, Scott disagreed with our growth figures, but that's hardly surprising. He wasn't terribly impressed with your performance either.

 Oh, right. That doesn't sound good. What did he say?

 He didn't think you came across very well and said that you lacked oomph. We should talk when we get a moment. I'm out all day now, but maybe tomorrow?

Everything about this is wrong, and it's another example of Harry not thinking things through. There's no problem with him giving Andy the news that they didn't get the funding, but he's selected the wrong time and place to give personal feedback. Whenever you need to have a difficult conversation, you have some choices about where and when to give it. Your options are:

- Here and now
- Here and later

- Somewhere else and now
- Somewhere else and later.

If Harry can take a second to think about the best option, he might choose to sit down with Andy over a coffee when they have an hour free later in the week. What's more, he'll be able to mull over how to tackle the conversation before they meet up. Harry rates Andy very highly for his financial savvy, but it's true that Andy doesn't always communicate well. Bearing this in mind, Harry might open things by asking how he feels the pitch went. Andy can then admit that it wasn't his best display, and this makes it easy for Harry for pick up the conversation:

> Andy, you bring fantastic strengths in terms of your financial skills, and I value those massively. One of the comments from our meeting with Scott was that you didn't come across as a natural communicator. He also said you lacked oomph, but this comment is so broad, I don't think it's particularly helpful. First I'd be keen to hear your thoughts, and then I have some specific feedback of my own.

By setting the context, Harry defuses Andy's fight-or-flight instincts and creates space for Andy to talk honestly about his strengths and weaknesses. Harry also gives feedback, but makes sure that his input is specific and behavioural rather than vague and general:

I know it's a small point, but you almost apologized when he questioned the five-year forecasts and I didn't think you needed to. I'd like you to have more conviction in your numbers when challenged.

Yes, I noticed myself doing exactly that. I'm not sure why, but I don't always stand up for myself.

If Harry follows the example of Zoe on pages 133–4 and asks brilliant questions, Andy will come out of the meeting feeling validated but also with a commitment to improve.

CLEAR UP THE MESS

There are times when, for whatever reason, we end up in the Bad Place or the Lock Down and face the problem of how to restore our relationship. Earlier we saw how project manager Rafa arranged to visit Liu Wei at their outsourcing business in China. Now Liu Wei is accompanying the vice-president of his company when he comes to the UK, and they make a late change to their itinerary that gives Rafa a week's warning of their arrival. When Liu Wei sends an email announcing a new date for the meeting – as if Rafa has nothing in his diary already – Rafa is irritated by their lack of consideration for his own schedule, and drops his chatty tone when he replies:

I'm not available that day and can't accommodate a late change to your plans.

Liu Wei ignores Rafa's email and they both end up in the Bad Place. Their conversation goes wrong because of what's unsaid as well as what's said. Liu Wei is deeply offended by what he perceives to be the disrespectful tone of Rafa's email; after all, he is arranging for the vice-president of his company to visit.

The disagreement between Rafa and Liu Wei is partly caused by different cultural norms, but they could have avoided Escalation by switching channel and picking up the phone. Rafa has a legitimate excuse for not being available on the date Liu Wei proposed – he is speaking at an industry conference – and believes he's done nothing wrong. Even so, he knows that he could have asked his boss to host the Chinese delegation, if only he was in the mood to do so. After some reflection, he makes efforts to call Liu Wei with the aim of clearing things up:

> I think my tone in my email may have offended you. If so, I fully apologize.

> Thank you, Rafa. I was upset. In our culture, it's essential to show respect. This visit is personally important to me and I need your help. Is there anyone that could meet my VP?

Rafa doesn't fully realize it, but Liu Wei is giving him the chance to save face and salvage the relationship. What's important is that Rafa has dropped his self-righteous tone. Some people may think that apologies have no place in the world of business, and Donald Trump famously said on NBC's *Tonight Show*: 'I fully think apologizing is a great thing. But you have to be wrong ... I will absolutely apologize sometime in the hopefully distant future, if I'm ever wrong.'[3]

Personally, I've lost count of the number of times I've had to resolve an issue that I've caused. It's not easy to address a problem and take responsibility for my part in it, but it always amazes me how an apology transcends differences in culture, age and gender. In contrast, denial and self-righteous indignation earn little respect.

WHAT TO DO?

STEP 1:
Distinguish Between Intent and Impact

The situation between Rafa and Liu Wei needn't have escalated if they'd distinguished between intent and impact. We are liable to take offence when none is intended, blaming the other person for their poor behaviour or flawed character rather than assuming that their words came out wrong or that they didn't mean to touch a nerve. The more upset we are, the more we feel that they are culpable. But this is faulty logic. Maybe part of the issue is our interpretation of what the other person said.

If Rafa and Liu Wei had recognized this, they could have avoided the Bad Place or the Lock Down. They could learn a lesson from Martha. By making a clear distinction in her mind between impact and intent, she rarely ends up in the Bad Place when people are abrasive.

In practice, you need to notice when you feel offended and remind yourself that the other person probably didn't seek to offend you. This can prevent you needlessly getting stuck in Blamestorming.

STEP 2:
Stay Aware of Your Values and Commitments

When you're having a difficult conversation, keep asking yourself what's important to you. As your emotions flow, it's easy to lose sight of your values, and this is why we say ridiculous things to the people we love, or fire back email replies that make us cringe later. If you can keep sight of what's important to you in these moments, instead of falling into Blamestorming, you'll make different choices in the heat of the moment.

I heard Sir Jackie Stewart telling the story of how he arrived at a race in the US where a huge old oak tree towered over the track. Unwilling to put himself or his fellow drivers at risk, he requested that the tree be cut down before the race. The track owner declined, saying it was a ludicrous request and pointing out that the tree pre-dated the track. Unwilling to compromise his values, Stewart decided not to race. Moaning and groaning, the marshals eventually cut down the tree on the morning of the race, but left a short stump. This prompted another difficult conversation, in which Stewart insisted that the stump needed to come out too. You can imagine the reaction to this request, but the stump was removed after further protestations. Stewart was in pole position on the starting grid, with fellow driver Denny Hulme alongside him. On the first lap, Hulme flew off the track on the outside of a corner at 180mph and drove straight over where the tree had been, but walked away with his life. Jackie's intervention reminds us that finding your voice can be the difference between disaster and redemption. 'You've got to do the right thing, however difficult the conversation,' he says.

There's nothing more powerful than a values-driven conversation in which you're clear where you stand without being self-righteous. By referencing your values under pressure, you have a better chance of responding mindfully to disagreement, challenge or provocation. When you're Stacking, Spinning, Skimming and Spilling, your values are the last thing on your mind.

Lesson 17: Notice your thoughts and feelings. Remain grounded in your values and commitments.

Chapter 18

INVENT The FUTURE

HOW TO CREATE NEW POSSIBILITIES THROUGH CONVERSATION

THE DIGITAL WAVE

In 1975, a young engineer called Steven Sasson presented a world-changing idea to his bosses but couldn't get anyone to listen. Scavenging components from his company's 'used parts' bin, he'd invented a contraption weighing 3.6 kg (8lb) that looked to any casual observer like a cassette recorder stuck on the side of a metal box with circuit boards and nickel cadmium batteries strapped underneath, and an old camera lens taped to the front. This was the world's first digital camera and it took 50 milliseconds to capture an image but 23 seconds to record the image onto a cassette tape, producing a 100 x 100 pixel black-and-white image.

Sasson demonstrated his device to the great and the good in his company and predicted that it would create a digital revolution. But there was a problem, and it was a big one. He worked for Kodak, the world's greatest photographic company, which made its money selling Kodak cameras loaded with Kodak film that was processed with Kodak chemicals and printed on Kodak paper. To put this in context, Kodak commanded 90 per cent of film sales and 85 per cent of camera sales in the US in the mid-1980s, and along came Sasson with a story that didn't involve film, chemicals or paper.

Terrified by the prospect that Sasson's invention would cannibalize their monopoly, his bosses blocked their ears and told him to keep his mouth shut. They allowed him to keep developing his camera so that they could register the patent, but there was a condition attached: he was instructed to hide it from the world. Kodak did eventually extract income from the patent but missed the chance to lead the market and watched their traditional business fall down a hole. They filed for bankruptcy in 2012 before relisting in late 2013.

NURTURING BARELY FORMED THOUGHTS

Now let's compare this to the story of Apple, co-founded by Steve Jobs and Steve Wozniak in 1976. Having been forced out of Apple in 1985, Jobs returned to the beleaguered company 12 years later and promptly started nurturing crazy-sounding ideas. He developed a campaign called 'Think Different' – taking the wind out of IBM's motto 'Think' – and Apple launched the new iMac in January 1999 in five flavours: tangerine, lime, blueberry, strawberry and grape. To grasp how radical this idea was, how would you feel about buying a flavoured car or television? It sounds nuts, but it's exactly what Apple did.

Much has been made of Steve Jobs' abrasive manner, but his ability to have conversations that invented new futures is not in question. Jobs and his chief design officer Jonathan Ive understood that ideas get developed through speaking and listening. That's why, when asked about the secret of innovation at Apple, Jobs didn't give a fancy reply about having robust structures and systems. Instead he said, 'Innovation comes from people meeting up in the hallways or calling each other at ten-thirty at night with a new idea, or because they realized something that shoots holes in how we've been thinking about a problem.'[1]

Jobs and Ive didn't subscribe to the idea that talk is cheap. Their interactions were integral to the creative process. In fact, during the early stages of product design, their conversation *was* the creative process. Here's how Ive expressed their partnership at Jobs's memorial service in 2011:

> *Steve used to say to me, and he used to say this a lot,*
> *'Hey, Jony, here's a dopey idea.' And sometimes they were*
> *really dopey. Sometimes they were truly dreadful. But*
> *sometimes they took the air from the room, and they left*
> *us both completely silent. Bold, crazy, magnificent ideas.*

> *Or quiet, simple ones which, in their subtlety, their detail,*
> *were utterly profound. And just as Steve loved ideas and*
> *loved making stuff, he treated the process of creativity with*
> *a rare and a wonderful reverence. You see I think he, better*
> *than anyone, understood that while ideas ultimately can be*
> *so powerful, they begin as fragile, barely formed thoughts,*
> *so easily missed, so easily compromised, so easily just*
> *squished. You know, I loved the way that he listened so*
> *intently, I loved his perception, his remarkable sensitivity*
> *and his surgically precise opinion.*[2]

There's a crucial point here. In your workplace, how many barely formed thoughts are missed because there's no one listening? How many are compromised, like Sasson's digital camera, because people are quick to introduce their concerns and complications? And how many are squished because people are more committed to explaining how it will never work rather than listening for a small spark of possibility?

IT ALL STARTS WITH CONVERSATION

It's all very well inventing the future if you're the world's biggest organization, but what if you're starting out from scratch, or own a one-person company operating from your back bedroom, or work for a small charity that's strapped for cash? Whatever your situation, you can invent a future that's appropriate to your circumstances, and it starts with conversation.

In 2003, having spent many years working in the advertising industry, Duncan Goose was pondering how to spend the next phase of his life when he met a group of friends in the Slug and Lettuce pub in Wardour Street, London. As they talked, it was mentioned that a billion people in the world don't have access to clean water, and a new idea was created that night: to launch a brand of bottled water called One, whose profits would fund clean-water projects in the world's poorest countries.

Goose recognized that ideas are fragile and conversations have a half-life unless you can build a structure around them. For this reason, he needed support, encouragement and constant prodding from a small group of committed allies and partners. Two years and hundreds of conversations later, he watched the first bottles of One roll off the production line. As he did so, Bob Geldof could be heard on the radio announcing Live 8, a music festival that would broadcast globally and campaign for leaders of G8 countries to increase aid efforts to developing nations. As Goose listened, a friend rang him and said, 'You've got to make One the official water for Live 8.'

Goose immediately filled his car up with bottles of water, drove back to London, and created a story to tell the three people who could make his idea a reality: Bob Geldof; Harvey Goldsmith, who produced Live Aid; and the writer and producer Richard Curtis. His plan was to drive to their respective offices, delivering his bottles of One and telling his story of opportunity. Before he'd reached the third office, Geldof, Goldsmith and Curtis had spoken to each other and endorsed his idea. One became the official water for Live 8 and was promoted on stage by Brad Pitt to an audience of over a billion people before they'd ever sold a bottle.

Since then, the One Foundation has raised $20 million for water projects that have contributed to over 3 million people. Always looking to raise the bar, Goose and his team have developed a crazy idea to raise 1 cent per litre from every bottle of water sold globally, and ended up pitching it to the United Nations General Assembly. Their plan would create $3 billion a year to support the eradication of water scarcity. Duncan Goose's most powerful asset is his ability to speak and listen.

THE POWER OF CONTEXT

Far from thoughts of Apple or Live 8, Oona is struggling with unacceptable store sales and knows that her days are numbered unless she and her staff can find some inspiration. But she doesn't know where to look for it. Her store's in need of a refit, and it's not on the high street, but it does sell excellent running gear and appeals to people who don't want to buy their kit online.

More in hope than expectation, Oona rallies her staff to come in for a couple of hours one evening after closing time and organizes pizza and a few beers. It's no small feat to bring them together because some of them have been serving customers all day and the off-duty staff need to travel in from home.

Oona sets the context well, asking her team to have a different kind of conversation:

> I'm very grateful to you for giving up your evening. We all know that times are pretty tough at the moment, and we're struggling on sales, but it's not for want of trying. The key lies in local marketing. None of us wants to do house-to-house leafleting, so let's rule that out. We need to create something more exciting, more meaningful. I've no idea what the answer is, but that's what we're here for. Please don't rule out or dismiss anyone's idea, even if you think it's ridiculous. And please listen!

It all starts off a bit slowly. There are several lacklustre variations on the leafleting approach, but at least nobody ridicules their colleague's idea. Finally Ben speaks up:

> I want to create a running movement.

It's one of those moments that Jonathan Ive described, when an idea takes the air out of the room. Everyone looks up from their slices of pizza and their beer bottles. They're not quite sure what Ben means, but it sounds intriguing, and he goes on to explain:

> If you think about it, the club runners and gym members already run at their clubs. But lots of people come in to buy kit and then run on their own. Why don't we create a running movement? We can promote it when customers come into the store, and we can run with them one evening a week after closing time. I don't mind organizing it.

Something rather amazing happens at this point. The context for their conversation has shifted: rather than selling kit, they are exploring how to create a movement. And instead of weighing in with their opinions, they consider what's needed to make Ben's idea fly. Kate says she's got a friend who owns a print company and could produce branded running vests at a moderate cost. Oona says she'll speak to regional manager Jack about creating a small marketing budget. Someone else says they'll set up a spreadsheet to record people's details and send out email reminders.

The first week it's only the staff who run, and some of them wonder if they've gone mad. On the second week two customers join them, after which Ben brings a few mates to help swell the numbers. More importantly perhaps, the two people who came in the second week have returned with a couple of friends. After a month of inviting every customer who comes into the shop, they reach 30 runners and celebrate as if they've won the lottery, with more beer and pizza. Thanks to the marketing department at head office, every runner gets a redeemable store voucher when they've completed their third run. The turning point is when an article appears in the local press, after which attendance doubles and people suddenly start to feel as if they're part of a movement. After three months, 60 people are running in two different groups. The faster group goes off first, and everyone else follows five minutes behind. Once they've finished the run, there's an open invitation to meet at the pub. A community has been formed, and sales are up by over 25 per cent.

Over the last couple of decades I've been in the privileged position of witnessing many similar conversations. Sometimes the challenge was to convert monolithic organizations into modern enterprises. On other occasions people took laughable ideas and turned them into propositions that captured a new market. Still others have transformed the lives of people in vulnerable communities, schools and hospitals.

WHAT TO DO?

STEP 1:
Develop a Thinking Environment

To invent the future you have to create some breathing space for a different kind of conversation. Things to consider are:

- **Choose your environment**: It's no coincidence that Apple's design meetings are held in the kitchen rather than round a boardroom table, or that the idea for One was born in a Slug and Lettuce pub. Some of the most creative conversations I've experienced have taken place in remote places with no wi-fi. Oona doesn't have the chance to take her team away, but at least she organizes beer and pizza.

- **Set the context**: Instead of saying, 'We need to get sales up' and then handing the conversation over to the floor, Oona creates a frame for their conversation, giving it a purpose and intention. She asks her team to respect each other's ideas, but also makes it clear that she trusts them to come up with the solution. The context you set will always shape how people think and participate.

- **Set up agreements**: You're wasting your time if you allow people to drift into Blamestorming, Dominatricks and Yes, But ... because they'll only get frustrated. Instead, create some ground rules together. This gives you a reference point that you can keep coming back to. Rule number one is to put away your devices. If people can't stop checking their messages, they're better off somewhere else.

- **Keep it tight**: Most world-beating ideas start off with a small group of people. Sometimes it's easier to share ideas with a smaller group, before everyone joins the conversation. It's only later that you'll want to involve the whole world in it. You may have seen or heard the story of Apollo 13, in which NASA's flight director Gene Kranz and his team had the seemingly impossible job of getting the astronauts back home after an explosion left them stranded in space and running out of power, water and oxygen. The ground crew had a few hours to put together a set of procedures that would normally take weeks to work out, operating outside all known design and test boundaries. In his book *Failure Is Not an Option*, Kranz recalls that he convened an emergency meeting of his staff. Rather than getting straight down to business, he announced that the room was too full to get anything done, and people left voluntarily to aid the thinking process of a smaller team.[3] By keeping your early conversations to a tight-knit group, you have a better chance of success.

- **Voice your ideas, and listen**: As Jonathan Ive said, even if an idea turns out to be a dopey one, you have to start by speaking it and being willing to listen. Long moments of silence characterize Ive's creative meetings, allowing time for people to think.

Notice that there's no place for Skimming and Spinning in a thinking environment. Your job is to create space for possibilities to emerge and, when they do, it's often the product of making random connections and hanging out in conversations that don't seem to be going anywhere.

STEP 2
Stay in the Conversation

Creating a possibility is just the start. Possibilities vanish as quickly as they appear if you don't nurture them, which is why the majority of New Year's resolutions are dropped within a couple of days. These are the principles to keep in mind:

- **Nurture your idea**: Oona and her staff keep the momentum going by discussing their running project in their staff meeting each morning, and again before closing the store in the evening. The lifeblood of this process is conversation. Jonathan Ive referred to the initial development work on the Apple watch as the 'watch conversation', which would have involved days, weeks and months of bashing ideas around, scribbling pencil drawings, having moments of revelation and getting stuck in dead ends. It was only in the autumn of 2011 that the 'watch conversation' transitioned into being a formal 'watch project'.

- **Keep asking what's needed**: The bigger your idea, the more obstacles you'll face and the more vocal your critics will be. For this reason, you want partners who are less interested in why it won't work and more interested in what's needed to make it fly. Every time a critic tells you why it'll fail, listen to the reason they give and ask yourself what's needed to overcome it. In this way, the naysayers help you to identify pitfalls and sharpen your thinking.

- **Hold each other to account**: If you take on a commitment, tell people to remind, prod and hold you to account for it. This doesn't mean that they'll snipe in your ear all day, but instead they'll offer encouragement, ask whether you've done what you promised, and challenge your assumptions on a regular basis. The truth is that you're far more likely to do something if you've told people you will.

- **Give up on control**: Inventing anything and bringing it to fruition in the world is a creative process and will be messy and chaotic at times. If you try to control it, you'll risk squeezing the life out of it. Since Ben came up with the idea of starting a running movement, Oona has empowered him to take the lead rather than trying to take personal control of it. Equally, Ben allows the rest of the team to contribute rather than getting overly possessive and protective. To make an idea succeed, you need to be willing to give it away. If you hold on to it too tightly, you'll extinguish it.

- **Create a movement**: If you're running a project, raising money for a charity or leading a business, try thinking of it as a movement and create a compelling story around it. When they take this on, the experience of coming to work is completely different for Ben, Oona and their colleagues. They're no longer just managing a running store or trying to sell gear. They're bringing together like-minded individuals, helping people get fit and creating a force for good in the world. People will buy more running kit as a natural consequence.

- **Acknowledge progress**: Finally, you need to celebrate progress as you go along, which gives you a boost and helps you stay in the game. More pizza and beer, then.

Lesson 18: Talk isn't cheap. It creates your future.

CONCLUSION

RIDING THE WAVES OF CHANGE

In every age, people have struggled to adapt to the pace of change. The 15th-century German Benedictine abbot Johannes Trithemius railed against the printing press, giving doomsday predictions that 'faith would weaken, charity would freeze, hope would die, law would perish, scripture fall into oblivion'.[1] He was right to fear for the future employment of scribes, but in fact the printing press made scriptures accessible to a global audience and, by the late 15th century, even the monasteries had created their own print houses.

Several centuries later, Alexander Graham Bell sought investment to exploit his new telephone invention and offered the patent to William Orton, president of the Western Union Telegraph Company, for $100,000. Orton, who was considered to be the foremost electrical expert in the country, could see no value in it: 'There is nothing in this patent whatever, nor is there anything in the scheme itself, except as a toy.'[2] Two years later, in 1878, Western Union realized they'd made an almighty mistake and would have been glad to pay $25 million for it, but the opportunity was gone and they were left to regret their lack of foresight.

Fast-forwarding another 110 years, I remember the day when I first saw a mobile phone being used and I reacted in the same way as Trithemius and Orton. A group of us were sitting in a meeting and were startled to hear a noise coming from under someone's chair. After unzipping a large bag, our colleague produced a brick-sized device, held it next to his ear and immediately got cut off from his caller while we roared with laughter. 'Is this the future?' we asked. It most certainly was.

As new technological waves crash over us again and again, and the prevailing tide pulls us toward Stacking, Spinning, Skimming and Spilling, it's our responsibility to ensure that we don't forget how to express our humanity through our conversations.

THE WAY FORWARD

Expecting perfection is the enemy of improvement – conversation is too messy for that – but we can take on a commitment to observe, practise and learn where to focus our attention. For example:

- If your attention is on the last conversation or the next one, you'll compromise the quality of the conversation you're in now.
- If you think you've got to say the 'right thing', you'll sacrifice your self-expression.
- If you're fixated with your version of the truth, you'll have no tolerance to hear someone else's story.
- If you're obsessed with following your pre-prepared script, you'll be thrown off-balance when the conversation takes an unexpected detour.
- If your chief concern is to be liked, you'll always steer clear of tricky conversations.
- If your attention is on self-protection, you'll automatically resort to Blamestorming when you're under pressure.

The good news is that you can choose where to focus your attention in each and every interaction. Here are three fundamental principles you can concentrate on in any conversation. Like the needle on a compass, they will keep you on track:

[1] Focus on Contribution

A few years ago, a friend of mine gave up his job as director of operations for a FTSE 100 company to fulfil his long-standing ambition to be a history teacher. His decision required a large dose of courage and a willingness to drop several steps down the income ladder, but he took the plunge and soon found himself working in a large secondary school. After a single term he went back to his old job. I asked him why things hadn't worked out, and he described the dispiriting atmosphere in the staff room. Quite simply, his colleagues were worn out, and the joy of contributing to their students – which had initially brought them into teaching – had been lost in the relentless battle to control their classrooms and meet their exam targets.

I've met many people who lost their focus on contribution or couldn't find it in the first place. When our day becomes about relying on our survival strategies to get through our to-do list, we forget that our job is to contribute to our customers, clients, patients, students, shareholders or constituents. In this way, coping and contribution aren't compatible. If we can restore our sense of purpose and meaning, our work suddenly becomes an opportunity for self-expression. The best way to address this is by viewing your day as a series of conversations in which you aim to put contribution at the heart of each interaction. Small moments of contribution can have momentous consequences.

[2] Trust Yourself

I recently worked with a business that was undergoing a huge IT transformation. Under immense pressure to migrate their customer data onto a new system, its leaders asked me to help design a launch meeting with 40 members of their technology team to communicate the plan for the next phase. I asked how they'd normally run a meeting like this and they said, 'We'd do a three-hour PowerPoint.' I suggested reversing their ratio of speaking to listening, meaning that their staff would do the majority of the talking. They glanced at each other and fidgeted. 'What would they talk about?' one of them asked. 'Let's hear their concerns and questions, and then draw on their expertise to help shape the plan,' I replied. 'After all, they're the ones who'll be delivering it.'

By now they were looking at me through narrowed eyes, as if I'd told them to run naked through the office. The problem for these leaders was that they didn't trust their ability to have an authentic conversation with their staff; it felt too scary. Of course, large groups can be intimidating but so can sales pitches, angry customers, disengaged colleagues, commercial negotiations, project-review meetings and difficult bosses. If only they could feel confident and equipped to deal with these situations, their experience at work would be very different. As it turned out, these leaders did have a genuine dialogue with their staff, who were delighted to discover they weren't going to be lectured. But the experience left me with a nagging question: 'Why isn't this the norm rather than the exception?'

The route to trusting conversation is through being present. You cannot listen to someone fully if you're Skimming, testing their words against your opinions, preparing to speak, thinking about the rest of your day or fretting about the direction your conversation might take. It's perfectly fine to have opinions, and to voice them too, but only after listening fully. As you become more present, your relationship to conversation shifts. You don't prepare so that you can say the right thing; you prepare so that you can be present in the interaction. You don't force conversations; you unfold them. As you experience the benefits of this approach, you learn to trust the process of conversation itself.

[3] Be a Learner

Hard as it is, we learn more from our failures than our successes. If we're honest with ourselves, we're all learners, and life has a way of humbling us if we think we've mastered it. As the great African-American poet Maya Angelou said, the most important thing we can learn is that we have so much to learn. We can also recognize that we face a choice in every conversation. We can be closed or be curious. Being closed leaves us less vulnerable but makes us righteous and defensive, always ready to blame someone or fight for our point of view. Being curious is more uncomfortable; it leaves us less certain, but more open to what life brings.

Most of us spend a huge proportion of our adult life in the workplace, and our greatest wish is to make it count. In truth, work *can* feel boring, frustrating, stressful and relentless at times. But if we can find our voice, and help other people to find theirs, it becomes an extraordinary opportunity for self-expression, collaboration, contribution and success. It's no exaggeration to say that each and every conversation offers the chance to leave another person feeling known, heard and empowered to make a difference. Often all we need is the courage to start a conversation and the humility to remember that we don't already know the answer.

TURN SMALL CHANGES INTO HABITS

Over time, the characters in *Workstorming* see real, tangible benefits from replacing mindless reactions with mindful responses that become habits. For example,

- Policy adviser Finn starts his new job, having negotiated favourable terms, and strives to take the second and third perspectives when facing a challenge.
- Entrepreneur Harry focuses on firing up his rational brain before reacting. If he's angry, he puts emails in his draft folder before sending them, or waits until he's cooled down and then picks up the phone.
- Regional retail manager Jack practises being in one conversation at a time. His finest moment is when his daughter Ellie tells him that he's listening slowly.
- Schoolteacher Lois takes on saying 'no' twice as often and stops being a victim of other people's requests. Far from seeing this as negative or obstructive, Matt trusts she'll deliver on her promises.
- Hospital volunteer Martha continues to be a blessing for visitors

to the intensive-care ward by listening, empathizing and establishing rapport with them.

- Maya and Lukas run a series of lunchtime seminars, encouraging their colleagues to value the merits of rapport-talk and report-talk.
- Project manager Rafa remembers that, while his team are testing code, he needs to be testing assumptions, and becomes his company's authority on working in China.
- Construction manager Sai remembers not to surrender his power, or his integrity, in the face of misplaced authority.
- Operations director Ria learns her lesson from Alex's resignation and makes it a priority to understand the motivations of the members of her team.
- Company owner Zoe shifts the ratio of questions to answers and watches how Ed and her other team members grow in stature, confidence and experience. As she lets go, she and her staff experience a new sense of freedom.

They all slip back into old habits and mindless reactions now and again, prompted by Stacking, Spinning, Skimming and Spilling. This makes them human. But, whatever their work throws at them, they're better equipped to find their voice and deal with the twists and turns of conversation, especially when they're under pressure.

My greatest hope is that *Workstorming* helps you trust in your ability to have *any* conversation, in *any* circumstance, with *anyone*. This doesn't mean you need a pre-prepared answer for every eventuality; it's quite the reverse. By being present in the conversation and trusting in the skills that you've developed, you'll stand a greater chance of saying something that makes a difference. If you're not sure of what to say, remember that your listening alone is powerful beyond measure.

While we don't know exactly what the future will hold, I feel confident of one thing: we'll invent it in conversation.

NOTES

Chapter 1

[1] See Steve Bradt, 'Wandering Mind Not a Happy Mind', *Harvard Gazette*, 11 November 2010, news.harvard.edu/gazette/story/2010/11/wandering-mind-not-a-happy-mind

Chapter 2

[1] Simon Jeffery, 'Adam Boulton harangues Alastair Campbell on Sky News', *Guardian*, 10 May 2010, www.theguardian.com/politics/blog/2010/may/10/adam-boulton-alastair-campbell

[2] Stephen Mihm, 'Dr. Doom', *New York Times Magazine*, 15 August 2008, www.nytimes.com/2008/08/17/magazine/17pessimist-t.html?_r=0

[3] See Cognisco, '$37 Billion – US and UK Businesses Count the Cost of Employee Misunderstanding', press release, 18 June 2008, www.marketwire.com/press-release/37-billion-us-and-uk-businesses-count-the-cost-of-employee-misunderstanding-870000.htm

Chapter 3

[1] See International Data Corporation (IDC), 'The Digital Universe of Opportunities: Rich Data and the Increasing Value of the Internet of Things', IDC white paper, 2014, www.idcdocserv.com/1678

[2] EMC, 'The Digital Universe of Opportunities: Rich Data and the Increasing Value of the Internet of Things', 2014, www.emc.com/leadership/digital-universe/2014iview/internet-of-things.htm

[3] Ministry of Defence, *Global Strategic Trends Out to 2045*, 5th Edition, 2014, www.gov.uk/government/uploads/system/uploads/attachment_data/file/348164/20140821_DCDC_GST_5_Web_Secured.pdf

[4] Ian Hardy, 'Losing Focus: Why Tech is Getting in the Way of Work', BBC News, 8 May 2015, www.bbc.co.uk/news/business-32628753, based on studies by Professor Gloria Mark, Donald Bren School of

Information and Computer Sciences, University of California.

[5] '"Infomania" Worse than Marijuana', BBC News, 22 April 2005, news.bbc.co.uk/1/hi/uk/4471607.stm

[6] Margie Warell, 'Combatting Attention Distraction Disorder: The Ultimate Tool', *Forbes*, 28 November 2012, www.forbes.com/sites/margiewarrell/2012/11/28/combatting-attention-distraction-disorder/#4975aee3ef82

[7] See the report by GFI Software quoted in 'Survey: Checking Email at Night, on Weekends and Holidays is the New Norm for US Workforce', PR Newswire, 14 May 2013, www.prnewswire.com/news-releases/survey-checking-email-at-night-on-weekends-and-holidays-is-the-new-norm-for-us-workforce-207352741.html

[8] The study was carried out by the Radicati Group, Inc., a US technology market-research firm, reported in Sheree Johnson, 'New Research Sheds Light on Daily Ad Exposures', *SJ Insights*, 29 September 2014, sjinsights.net/2014/09/29/new-research-sheds-light-on-daily-ad-exposures

[9] 'Adults Spend Almost 10 Hours a Day with the Media but Note Only 150 Ads', Media Dynamics Inc. press release, 22 September 2014, www.mediadynamicsinc.com/uploads/files/PR092214-Note-only-150-Ads-2mk.pdf

[10] According to 'The Great British Bedtime Report', a survey by Opinion Matters for the Sleep Council in 2013, www.sleepcouncil.org.uk/wp-content/uploads/2013/02/The-Great-British-Bedtime-Report.pdf

[11] Jeffrey M Jones, 'In US, 40% Get Less Than Recommended Amount of Sleep', based on 2013 Gallup poll conducted with 1,031 adults, www.gallup.com/poll/166553/less-recommended-amount-sleep.aspx

[12] Martin Hilbert, 'How Much Information is there in the "Information Society"?', *Significance*, vol. 9, no. 4 (2012), pp. 8–12, www.onlinelibrary.wiley.com/doi/10.1111/j.1740-9713.2012.00584.x/abstract

[13] 'Absence Management', Chartered Institute of Personal Development, Annual Survey Report, 2014, www.cipd.co.uk/binaries/absence-management_2014.pdf

[14] American Psychological Association, 'Work and Well-Being Survey, 2013', www.apaexcellence.org/assets/general/2013-work-and-wellbeing-survey-results.pdf

[15] See Sarah Glynn, 'Work is the Number One Cause of Stress, Suggests Study', *Medical News Today*, 20 March 2013, www.medicalnewstoday.com/articles/257889.php

[16] See Jeevan Vasagar, 'Out of Hours Working Banned by German Labour Ministry', *Daily Telegraph*, 30 August 2013, www.telegraph.co.uk/news/worldnews/europe/germany/10276815/Out-of-hours-working-banned-by-German-labour-ministry.html

Chapter 4

[1] Evian Gordon, 'NeuroLeadership and Integrative Neuroscience: "It's About Validation Stupid!"', *NeuroLeadership Journal*, vol. 1 (2008), www.acsg.co.za/archives/2013-icacm-and-acsg-conference/Emde_1_NeuroLeadership-and-Integrative.pdf

[2] Study by Halfords Autocentres reported in 'Motorists Filling Cars with Wrong Fuel Costs Britain £150m', *Mail on Sunday*, 21 October 2012, www.dailymail.co.uk/news/article-2220871/Motorists-filling-cars-wrong-fuel-costs-Britain-150m.html

[3] Reported in Lisa Evans, 'The Exact Amount of Time You Should Work Every Day', Fast Company website, 28 September 2014, www.fastcompany.com/3035605/how-to-be-a-success-at-everything/the-exact-amount-of-time-you-should-work-every-day

Chapter 5

[1] Henning Mankell, 'The Art of Listening', *New York Times*, 10 December 2011 (trans. Tina Nunnally), www.nytimes.com/2011/12/11/opinion/sunday/in-africa-the-art-of-listening.html?_r=0

[2] 'A Conversation Between Malala Yousafzai and World Bank Group President Jim Yong Kim', 11 October 2013, www.worldbank.org/en/news/speech/2013/10/11/transcript-malala-yousafzai-world-bank-group-president-jim-yong-kim

[3] See Gallup Q^{12} Meta-Analysis, strengths.gallup.com/private/resources/q12meta-analysis_flyer_gen_08%2008_bp.pdf

Chapter 6

[1] David Grady and Jason Fried, 'The Economic Impact of Bad Meetings', TED talk, 17 November 2014, ideas.ted.com/the-economic-impact-of-bad-meetings

[2] Michael C Mankins, 'This Weekly Meeting Took Up 300000 Hours a Year', *Harvard Business Review*, 29 April 2014, hbr.org/2014/04/how-a-weekly-meeting-took-up-300000-hours-a-year

[3] Lawrence Tobin, 'Sir Bradley Wiggins Out of 2014 Tour de France', *Independent*, 27 June 2014, www.independent.co.uk/sport/cycling/sir-bradley-wiggins-out-of-2014-tour-de-france-sir-dave-brailsford-confirms-he-will-not-be-part-of-9567880.html

Chapter 7

[1] See Jessica Gross, 'What Motivates Us at Work? More than Money', TED blog, 21 May 2015, ideas.ted.com/what-motivates-us-at-work-7-fascinating-studies-that-give-insights

Chapter 8

[1] D Kahneman, *Thinking Fast and Slow*, Farrar, Straus and Giroux, New York, 2011

[2] Conducted by McKinsey & Company and the BT Centre for Major Programme Management at the University of Oxford, 2012; see Michael Bloch, Sven Blumberg and Jurgen Laartz, 'Delivering Large-Scale IT Projects on Time, on Budget and on Value', McKinsey website, October 2012,

www.mckinsey.com/insights/business_technology/delivering_
large-scale_it_projects_on_time_on_budget_and_on_value

Chapter 9

[1] CK Hofling, ERN Brotzman, SRN Dalrymple, NRN Graves and CM Pierce, 'An Experimental Study in Nurse–Physician Relationships', *Journal of Nervous and Mental Disease*, vol. 143 (1966), pp. 171–80

[2] See 'Plane Crash Transcripts Published', Press Association, 2010, web.archive.org/web/20100605080110/http://www.google.com/hostednews/ukpress/article/ALeqM5j6nrwJeaqOWBTEwjIvhaCdcFgMRQ

[3] See Ian Johnston, 'Labour's Ed Stone Was a Mistake which Slipped Through 10 Election Meetings, Claims Report', *Independent*, 3 June 2015, www.independent.co.uk/news/uk/politics/labours-ed-stone-was-a-mistake-which-slipped-through-10-election-meetings-claims-report-10295929.html

Chapter 10

[1] Aristotle, *Nicomachaean Ethics*, Book 5, Chapter 10; see 1955 translation by WD Ross at classics.mit.edu/Aristotle/nicomachaen.5.v.html

Chapter 11

[1] Harvey Penick, *The Wisdom of Harvey Penick*, Simon & Schuster, London, 1997, pp. 137–8

[2] Peter Drucker, 'Marketing Challenges, Business Challenges, Management Challenges Facing the Coca-Cola Company in the Nineteen Nineties', report, December 1992, ccdl.libraries.claremont.edu/utils/getfile/collection/dac/id/3583/filename/4033.pdf

Chapter 12

[1] D Tannen, *Talking from 9 to 5: Women and Men at Work: Language, Sex and Power*, Virago Press, London, 1995, p. 115

[2] PM Fishman, 'Interaction: The Work Women Do', *Social Problems*, vol. 25, no. 4 (1978), pp. 397–406. Fishman's conclusions were based on 52 hours of tape-recorded conversations between intimates in their homes.

[3] B Annis and J Gray, *Work with Me: How Gender Intelligence Can Help You Succeed at Work and in Life*, Piatkus, London, 2013, p. 114

[4] Fishman, 'Interaction'

[5] See James W Pennebaker, 'Your Use of Pronouns Reveals Your Personality', *Harvard Business Review*, December 2011, and Bridget Kiely, 'The Secret Life of Pronouns', *Yale Scientific*, March 2012

[6] See Deborah Tannen, 'He Said, She Said', *Scientific American Mind*, May 2010

[7] Annis and Gray, *Work with Me*, p. 114

Chapter 13

[1] 'E-mail Error Ends Up on Road Sign', BBC News, 30 October 2008, news.bbc.co.uk/1/hi/7702913.stm

[2] Airline Pilots Association, 'Human Factors on the Tenerife Accident', project-tenerife.com/engels/PDF/alpa.pdf

[3] 'Final Report and Comments of the Netherlands Aviation Safety Board', published October 1978, www.faasafety.gov/files/gslac/courses/content/232/1081/finaldutchreport.pdf

Chapter 15

[1] For more information on Chinese cultural norms, read Jonathan Geldart, *Notes from a Beijing Coffee Shop,* Lid Publishing, London, 2015

[2] A Krishna, S Sahay and G Walsham, 'Managing Cross-Cultural Issues in Global Software Outsourcing', *Communications of the AMC*, vol. 47, no. 4 (2004), pp. 62–6

[3] Stephanie Pappas, 'East vs. West: Stark Coast-to-Coast Culture Clash Revealed', LiveScience website, 18 September 2012, www.livescience.com/23283-east-vs-west-coast-culture-differences.html

[4] Linda Milazzo, 'Newt Gingrich Declares, "I Am Not a Citizen of the World!"', *Huffington Post* blog, 10 July 2008, www.huffingtonpost.com/linda-milazzo/newt-gingrich-declares-i_b_212968.html

[5] KM Kniffen, B Wanskink, CM Devine and J Sobal, 'Eating Together at the Firehouse: How Workplace Commensality Relates to the Performance of Firefighters', *Human Performance*, vol. 28, no. 4 (2015), pp. 281–306

Chapter 16

[1] K Fox, *Watching the English*, Hodder and Stoughton, London, 2004

[2] 'Sir Alex Ferguson: The Secrets Behind his Success', BBC Sport website, 6 October 2015, www.bbc.co.uk/sport/0/football/34448977

Chapter 17

[1] Sir Jackie Stewart, *Winning is Not Enough*, Headline, London, 2007, p.146

[2] E Barker interview with Chris Voss, '6 Hostage Negotiation Techniques that Will Get You What You Want', *Time*, March 2014.

[3] See Ben Jacobs, 'Donald Trump on the Tonight Show: "I Will Apologize ... If I'm Ever Wrong"', *Guardian*, 12 September 2015, www.theguardian.com/us-news/2015/sep/12/donald-trump-on-the-tonight-show-i-will-apologize-if-im-ever-wrong

Chapter 18

[1] From an interview with Steve Jobs in *Business Week* in 2004, reprinted in 'Steve Jobs: In his Own Words', *Daily Telegraph*,

6 October 2011, www.telegraph.co.uk/technology/steve-jobs/
8811892/Steve-Jobs-in-his-own-words.html

[2] Philip Elmer-DeWitt, 'Jonathan Ives on Steve Jobs and the Fragility
of Ideas', *Fortune*, 24 October 2011, fortune.com/2011/10/24/
jonathan-ive-on-steve-jobs-and-the-fragility-of-ideas

[3] G Kranz, *Failure is Not an Option*, Berkley Publishing Group,
New York, 2001, p.320

Conclusion

[1] See excerpts from Johannes Trithemius, *In Praise of Scribes*,
at misc.yarinareth.net/trithemius.html

[2] Chauncey M Depew, *My Memories of Eighty Years*, Charles
Scribner's Sons, New York, 1922, www.gutenberg.org/
files/2045/2045-h/2045-h.htm#chap18

FURTHER READING

Annis, B and Gray, J, *Work with Me: How Gender Intelligence Can Help You Succeed at Work and in Life*, Piatkus, London, 2013

Duhigg, C, *The Power of Habit: Why We Do What We Do and How to Change*, Random House Books, London, 2012

Fox, K, *Watching the English*, Hodder and Stoughton, London, 2004

Geldart, J, *Notes from a Beijing Coffee Shop*, Lid Publishing, London, 2015

Kahneman, D, *Thinking Fast and Slow*, Farrar, Straus and Giroux, New York, 2011

Kendall, R, *Blamestorming: Why Conversations Go Wrong and How to Fix Them*, Watkins Pubishing, London, 2014

Langer, E, *Mindfulness*, 25th Anniversary Edition, Da Capo Press, Boston, 2014

Levitin, D, *The Organized Mind: Thinking Straight in the Age of Information Overload*, Penguin, London, 2015

Penick, H, *The Wisdom of Harvey Penick*, Simon & Schuster, London, 1997

Tannen, D, *Talking from 9 to 5: Women and Men at Work: Language, Sex and Power*, Virago Press, London, 1995

ACKNOWLEDGMENTS

Workstorming is the product of collaborating with many remarkable people over the last 25 years. I'm indebted to them for allowing me to learn and make mistakes, often at their expense. I'm especially grateful to the friends and colleagues who read my manuscript during its development and offered their expert input, and to my daughter Emily, who proved her superb research abilities.

I'm lucky to have the guidance of Robert Kirby at United Agents, and Fiona Robertson at Watkins. Fiona's support and encouragement have been as invaluable to me as her editorial skills. I've also benefited greatly from Jessica Cuthbert-Smith's copyediting and the contributions of Fra Corsini, Jo Lal and Vicky Hartley at Watkins.

Looking back, I don't remember ever being pressed to follow a career path during my school years. My parents encouraged me to develop an adventurous spirit and to head in the general direction of my passions, with allowance for plenty of zigzags. I can't think of better career advice.

Around the time I completed the manuscript for *Workstorming*, a consultant doctor faced a difficult conversation one Thursday morning. He told Elizabeth, an outpatient in her mid-eighties, that her stomach pains were worse than she'd feared and that there was no treatment available. That evening, with typical courage, Elizabeth called her family to tell them the news. Since Elizabeth was my mother, one of those calls was to me. The final weeks of her life required us to have hundreds of conversations with carers, consultants, doctors, nurses and night-sitters. Nobody who goes through this experience can argue that talk is cheap. During the course of her 40 years of work with disabled people and service to the community, thousands of people felt known, loved and appreciated after having a conversation with my mother. It was impossible to know her without feeling loved by her. She taught me how to listen slowly, and this book is for her.

My parents are not the only people whose generous listening I have been blessed with. My wife Sally has demonstrated oceans of it, and I'm eternally thankful to her; any accomplishments I can claim are really hers too. As for our children, Emily, Rosy and Marcus, they train us in communication on a daily basis. Most importantly, they make us happy. I couldn't ask for more.

ABOUT THE AUTHOR

By the age of 18, Rob had lived on four continents. An early lesson in communication came on leaving school, when he worked with amputees in India. Speaking no Hindi, he found a way of communicating with them through sign language and drawing portraits of them in his sketchbook. Returning to the UK, he completed a degree in English before deciding to be a professional artist. He had only one painting in his portfolio, but it was selected from 3,000 entries to sell in every IKEA store worldwide. Thus he enjoyed the fleeting accomplishment of outselling copies of Monet's *Water Lilies*!

Always looking for a new challenge, Rob became fascinated with understanding the dynamics of effective communication. Over the last 25 years he's applied these skills to co-launching a technology company, being a consultant to more than 70 organizations across five continents and being a Non-Executive Director of BAFTA- and EMMY-winning visual-effects company Jellyfish Pictures. Such eclectic career choices may appear to have little in common, but Rob would argue that they all involve conversation. He makes frequent radio appearances and writes a regular blog for *Psychology Today*.

Rob has been married to Sally for 25 years and has three children.

For more information, see: www.robkendall.co.uk and www.conversationexpert.com

ABOUT *BLAMESTORMING*

Do your disagreements often escalate into rows? Do you get crossed wires when talking to your stressed partner, difficult teenager, over-worked colleagues or demanding boss? If so, *Blamestorming* holds the answers for you.

Published in 2014, B*lamestorming: Why Conversations Go Wrong and How to Fix Them* explores conversations with our partners, children, parents, friends and colleagues. Packed with transcripts and practical examples, the book explains how to stop conversations becoming destructive arguments, how to prepare for and conduct challenging conversations, and how to reduce defensiveness in others. If you've enjoyed *Workstorming*, it's the perfect opportunity to take your learning further.

Blamestorming won the Coalition of Visionary Resources award for best 'how-to' book in the USA, was a finalist for the Small Business Book Awards, and reached number one on Amazon's 'Movers and Shakers' list.

WATKINS

Sharing Wisdom Since
1893

The story of Watkins dates back to 1893, when the scholar of esotericism John Watkins founded a bookshop, inspired by the lament of his friend and teacher Madame Blavatsky that there was nowhere in London to buy books on mysticism, occultism or metaphysics. That moment marked the birth of Watkins, soon to become the home of many of the leading lights of spiritual literature, including Carl Jung, Rudolf Steiner, Alice Bailey and Chögyam Trungpa.

Today our passion for vigorous questioning is still resolute. With over 350 titles on our list, Watkins Publishing reflects the development of spiritual thinking and new science over the past 120 years. We remain at the cutting edge, committed to publishing books that change lives.

DISCOVER MORE . . .

Read our blog

Watch and listen to
our authors in action

Sign up to
our mailing list

JOIN IN THE CONVERSATION

Our books celebrate conscious, passionate, wise and happy living.
Be part of the community by visiting

www.watkinspublishing.com